CW00468100

Mysterious Somerset

Unsolved Murders, Vanishing People and Local Legends

A M GOULD

ISBN 9781916394117

First Published in 2020 by author AM Gould

Copyright © 2020 A M Gould. All rights Reserved

Website amgouldsomersetauthor.com

All Rights Reserved. Apart from any permitted use under UK copyright law, no part of this publication may be reproduced or transmitted in any form or by any means electronic or mechanical, including photocopying, recording or any information, storage or retrieval system without permission in writing from the publisher or under licence from the Copyright Licensing Agency Limited. Further detail of such licences (for reprographic reproduction) may be obtained from the Copyright Licensing Agency Ltd, Saffron House, 6-10 Kirby Street, London EC1N 8TS

Table of Contents

Introduction

Like every county, the wonderful Somerset has certain locations, people and events that carry an air of mystery. The characteristics of local stories, people and places have been passed down through the generations. This book happened by accident whilst working on another project. A little bit of research and all of a sudden, I find these wonderful stories and I asked myself how have I, now in my 40s, and living only in Somerset, not come across these wonderful things? Centuries-old customs that local communities continue to keep alive, wonderful legends of fairies, dragons and beasts and stories attached to landmarks, mysterious murders, and strange people.

Whilst researching and writing this book I have spoken to many local people, who work hard to organise and carry out wonderful customs in their towns and villages. Some which date back to medieval times. The superstitions that our ancestors followed and practiced to understand and navigate the changing world are very much alive in us. There are many superstitions we share as a society and there are the wonderfully ones unique to us in Somerset. I didn't realise when locals stated that it always rained at Bridgwater Fair that this is actually a belief not a prediction, passed on from father to son for hundreds of years.

The second part of Mysterious Somerset shares stories of unsolved murders and mysterious people. There are many murders that have gone unpunished in Somerset. Some in which, to me, the culprit is fairly clear, but with no evidence to proof or disproof, the perpetrator literally got away with murder. There are also some where there simply is no explanation as to why people lost their lives. I will leave it to you, the reader, to draw your own conclusions as to whether a person's death was an accident or indeed a murder.

The chapter on mysterious people focus on people that carry some kind of mystery about them. People who vanish, never to return, leaving broken hearts and legal entanglements in their absence, people who arrive in the county with a dubious history or intention. Local celebrities who are loved by the community but mistrusted by the media and authorities. People who seem to display an incredible behaviour or skill which can never be proven or dismissed.

I would like to thank the many people who took the time to chat to me about their communities. The church wardens, schoolteachers, local volunteers, and charities who provided me with anecdotes, old images, and additional research materials. I would also like to thank the followers I have on Facebook who continue to engage with the history of Somerset and support and contribute to my storytelling. May we continue to keep the ancestors of Somerset alive in our minds.

Customs

Customs were once the backbone to all communities. From the universally shared celebrations to the more localised gatherings, customs have allowed people to join together to celebrate annual events. Even in these modern times, local customs are still celebrated annually, bringing together the residents of a community, who, in this busy society, can sometimes be quite detached from their neighbours. For this chapter, I have focused on the customs of Somerset towns and villages which are less known. We have the wonderful customs that are shared throughout our society, such as pancake tossing and maypole dancing. We have our popular county customs such as the Carnival and Bridgwater Fair. But the customs in this chapter are so marvellously unique to specific towns and villages. Just reading about them endears these communities to me for their individuality and community spirit. There is no doubt that only a town or village with a dedicated community would work together to ensure these customs remain in place for the generations to come. During my research, I have spoken to many local event holders who have told me of the pride their communities hold in keeping their local customs alive.

There are some customs detailed in this chapter, which, by today's standards of morality, would be unacceptable. There is a real moral question in today's society as to whether we remember and celebrate the behaviours and attitudes of historical events. Personally, I think it is important to recognise that although activities such as bull-baiting or skimmerton riding are no longer acceptable, these events and behaviours in our history shaped how society grew to condemn and abolish them, paving the way to a fairer, more humane society.

Candle Auctions

This custom of auction by candle is also known as a Dutch auction or 'selling by candle'. From the earliest records, candles were used as a way to measure time and this method of auction is believed to have been adopted from Holland. Candlelight auctions were a popular method of land auction throughout the 16th century and was advocated by Cromwell who deemed it a much fairer way to value land.

In the village of Chedzoy near Bridgwater, the custom of auctioning a piece of land through the candlelight dates back 500 years. An acre of arable land called Church Acre; property of the village church, is leased by candlelight auction every 21 years.

Image kindly provided by the church warden of Chedzoy

In 1490, a local man named Richard Sydenham, a large landowner, bequeathed this land to the church under the condition that the land would be auctioned by candle every 21 years and any profits given to the Church of St Mary in Chedzoy.

The auction would traditionally take place at a local village pub, The Manor being the location since 1904. The auction would involve the lighting of half an inch of candle, lit by the church rector. The candle would burn for around 30 minutes and during this time, locals would place their bids. Whoever bid as the candle extinguished itself was successful and would manage the land for the next 21 years. The event was typically attended by the Bishop of Bath and Wells and the church rector. The earliest recorded transaction took place in 1672 in which the land was won for £6, which is around £600 in today's money. The most recent auction was held in 2010 and the land fetched £4,000. The next auction will be held in April 2021.

In the village of Tatworth, two miles outside of Chard, a similar auction is held yearly to determine the annual tenant of a piece of land called Stowell Mead. This land is a meadow and watercress bed which consists of seven acres and sits near Forton Lane. The known origin of this custom dates back to 1832, however, it is thought to be much older. Legend tells that a disgruntled clerk destroyed older records. Before 1832, the land was shared by farmers who used it for pasture, however, the 1820 changes in land ownership legislation saw the piece of land become overcrowded with cattle. Locals needed to find an alternative way to decide fair use. The rights owners met and agreed they should rent the land out on a yearly basis with all rent being shared between the men. They formed a yearly meeting which they named the Stowell Court. This court met on the first Tuesday after the 6th April each year in a locked room in the Poppe Inn. Only members could attend, and any late arrivals were fined. Like Chedzoy, the court would light a small piece of tallow candle to begin proceedings. No one could leave their seat, cough, or sneeze so that the candle could burn down naturally. Once the candle went out and the winning bid was awarded, the rights owners would share this rent for the next year. After the auction, the court would enjoy a feast of breads, cheeses, and watercress and drink merrily into the night. In 1888, the Western Gazette described the land as a complete bog of little value. In fact, one tenant had to shoot his horse because it got stuck in the marshy field. The meadow was frequented often by locals and was locally complimented as having the best watercress around. The village continues to maintain the candle auction custom to the modern day. The longest ever burning candle is said to have been in 1805 when it burnt for seventy-six minutes and the shortest was recorded as just eighteen minutes.

In the villages of Puxton, Congresbury and Wick St Lawrence, an even more unusual ancient custom was used to determine who would be awarded the use of land in the area of the East and West Dolmoors. The process involved the measuring of land and a lottery of apples! On the first Saturday after Midsummer's day, local landowners were summoned to Puxton church by the ringing of the church bells. Once at the church, the chain that was used for measuring the land was checked and inspected by the landowners. The chain was 54 feet in length, which was

12 inches shorter than the standard acre, and its length was determined by measuring it from the foot of the church arch, down through the aisle and to the west door. Anyone who wished to check for tampering or mismeasure was granted permission to settle any suspicion. 24 apples were then selected, each marked in a particular way, which corresponded to each landowner. The apples were then placed in a bag or a hat and given to the chosen apple holder, normally a young lad from the community.

The two chosen measurers—the apple holding boy and a large number of spectators—then headed to the moors where the beginning of the land measure took place. Once an acre was achieved, the apple bringer would reach in to pull an apple. Whichever symbol was displayed on the apple was cut into the ground with a sickle and the landowner who bore that symbol would rent that piece of land for one year. Once the

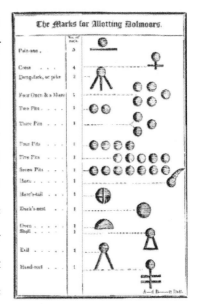

process was completed, the party would return to the home of one of the landowners and a candle auction would be carried out to determine the rental of certain allocated plots. In this auction, the piece of land was named, and an interested party would name his bid and place a shilling on the table. The candle was then lit, and others were permitted to outbid him. If outbid, the person would need to remove their shilling and place it back on the table with a higher bid. This went on until the candle extinguished itself.

Once the candle auction was complete, the locals would enjoy a huge celebration with bread, butter, cheese, ale, and tobacco. Only locals could attend the revel and any outsiders would have to pay a fine of one shilling to join the celebrations. Fuelled by ale and excitement, these celebrations could become rowdy, with friendly fights and rough housing. On many occasions, efforts were made to bring a stop to the custom, however, it continued until 1810 when the land ownership laws enclosed the land.

Beating of the Bounds

Another example of a land-relating custom carried out by locals was the act of the beating of the bounds. It is important to say this was not a Somerset specific custom but one that many Somerset towns and villages thoroughly enjoyed. Beating the bounds is an ancient custom, believed to date back to Anglo-Saxon times in which prominent people would walk the boundaries of their parish on Ascension Day (13th May). Using boughs of ash or willow they would walk to the edges of their parish beating the boundary markers. The original purpose of this action is thought to be to ensure boundaries from neighbouring parishes remained in their correct place. Parish boundaries prevented disputes over costs, who the poor belonged to, or who should be buried in which parish.

An account of the ascension in the parish of Wells from 1752 indicates that during earlier times, boys were whipped at the boundary markers and sixpences thrown over the side of bridges. In this account, the mayor, vicar, town clerk, church warden, and locals set off together walking through the parish, stopping at local boundary markers to whip local people that had misbehaved or used foul language. In more recent times, the custom has been less violent and more about bringing a community together. Younger boys were armed with boughs of wood which they would use to mark the boundaries.

Boundary marker, Selwood, South Somerset

Once the custom was carried out, the local community would enjoy a celebration in which they were given parish ale. The custom of beating the bounds has been continued into modern times in Wellington, carried out by local scout troops and town councillors.

Clipping the Church

Clipping the church or tower is an ancient custom believed to originate from the Pagans. This custom was carried out across Somerset into the 19th century but is not unique to the county or to England, it is a tradition that was carried out around the world. Each year, the local people would gather at the village churchyard. Sometimes on the Saint's day of said church and sometimes on Midsummer's day. Forming a circle around the church, they would hold hands and dance, gradually moving toward the building. The two people near the church door would break the circle and lead the others down to the church yard gates and into the streets.

Continuing in a line, the party would dance through the street with one member 'threading the needle' – running in a zig-zag direction through the line. Once they reached the village green, they would give three loud shouts to frighten the devil away from the parish. This excited crowd would then proceed onto a three-day celebration named the revels.

Clipping the Church at Rode, Somerset by W.W Wheatley, 1848

The Somerset Revels

The annual revels were another ancient custom in the county of Somerset. These social gatherings were held in most Somerset villages around Midsummer's day, although could also take place after Easter or on the Saint's day of their local church. A village revel would normally take place on the church or village green and run for three days. The celebrations were filled with alcohol, wrestling, cudgel playing (fighting with wooden staffs), and other rowdy games.

In July 1650, a man named Thomas George tried to halt the Langford Budville revels by attending the village with other men with a warrant. When he arrived, he found over sixty people gathered on the church green, many were inebriated and engaging in rough contact sports and boisterous merriment. George read his warrant to the crowd and a reveller immediately challenged him, asking why he thought he had the right to tell them to stop. He declared if a fight was what he came for, then that is what he would get. A brawl then ensued, and Thomas George was hanged from a tree while his company were beaten badly.

Later, celebrations were more respectful of the law, and by the 1800s, constables only made an invisible presence unless arrests were required. The 19th century revels still featured the aggressive but friendly fighting games but also featured stalls offering refreshments and local dancing groups performing routines to entertain the spectators. During the period of celebration, women who were in service with local families could return home to their loved ones and employee's duties were relaxed. The duration of the revel was enjoyed with singing local folk songs and eating and drinking to precarious levels.

In Huish Episcopi, the prizes included a ram for winning at wrestling, a beaver hat for the most grotesque face pulled, and if you were able to climb up a greasy pole, you could have the ham that sat at the top. In

West Somerset, the revels included bull-baiting and cock fighting, while in Long Sutton, the men would hold free bare-knuckle fights with the villagers of neighbouring Long Load. The local police would have to attend regularly at these events and officials wanted them banned.

The annual revel of Thurloxton was permanently abolished in 1850 when the chaos of the celebrations was held responsible for a terrible accident. Mr and Mrs Westcombe, returning from Bridgwater to Adsborough, were travelling along the Bridgwater to Taunton road. As they approached the Green Dragon where the locals had gathered for the revels, the noise of the celebration allegedly frightened the horse, causing it to dart, tipping the coach and throwing the couple from their carriage. Mrs Westcombe broke her thigh bone and her husband had a serious head injury. Fortunately, both recovered. Eventually, all local revels were ended toward the late 19th century when it was alleged that a Jewish man was murdered and buried, the culprit then escaping the area. In some locations such as Butleigh near Glastonbury, the revels continued in the 1900's but it was no doubt more like a fete with much more decorum and much less alcohol and fighting.

The Ashen Faggot

The burning of the ashen faggot is an old west country custom, which, although not singular to Somerset, has always been carried out alongside wassailing, especially in the West of the county. The ashen faggot can be likened to the modern-day Yule log and consisted of a large bundle of ash twigs, around five foot in length, tied together with nine lengths of ash bind, preferably from the same tree, which is then burnt on Christmas Eve in the fireplace as a family celebration of the festive period. The origins of the practice are disputed, some saying it dates back to the Norse mythology's idolisation of the Ash Tree. An alternative origin is that the practise was taken from Alfred the Great's time hidden in the Somerset marshes, in which the soldiers created these bundles to stay warm on the eve of the battle Ethandune. The Christian explanation states that the custom comes from Virgin Mary's time in a cold stable, and that Joseph gathered and lit bundles of ash to keep her warm whilst the saviour was born.

However the custom began, the burning of the ashen faggot was an important part of Christmas celebrations for most rural Somerset communities in times gone by. The tradition dictated that the family would gather and tie the faggot with nine binds, then the oldest member of the family would carry the bundle into the house and place it into the fireplace. The remains of last year's faggot would then be used to ignite the new one and the merriment would begin. The burning ash would create a lot of flame and crackling, and each time one of the nine binds broke, the family would raise a toast.

The older members of the household would partake in a cobblers punch—a mixture of cider and gin, whilst the younger ones preferred a cider-nog, a mixture of cider, eggs, and cream.

The gathering of the Ashen Faggot- Granger 1854

While the faggot was burning, all members of the household were of the same station, with servants and farm hands dancing and singing with their employers in a manner never entertained at any other time. Games such as sack races and apple bobbing were enjoyed along with traditional ashen faggot songs. These songs were recited from the memory of the people and rarely recorded on paper. Misfortune was predicted for any household that did not follow this tradition.

Wassailing the Trees

The tradition of wassailing is an ancient custom which is believed to originate from the Anglo-Saxons, the word wassailing meaning 'be in good health'. The custom has two strands, the first was to visit homes with a spiced drink in a bowl, to knock at the door and to receive gifts from the household in return for a Christmas drink and a wish of good luck for the upcoming year. This custom seems to have been replaced by the more Christian tradition of carol singing and gathering alms for the poor in 12th century England. The wassailing home visits were a popular way for the lord of the manor to give his thanks to his hard-working tenants. Many out visiting homes would provide a little dance to an accordion to entertain the family. Refusal to offer a donation to these seasonal well-wishers could result in a curse being placed upon the home. Like modern times with carol singers, some people found wassailing at their door vulgar and an excuse for rowdy people to demand food and drink from their wealthy neighbours. The adaption by the Christian faith to carol singing, with religious songs and donations for the needy, made this custom much more acceptable to the higher members of society and the church.

The second strand of wassailing is to give thanks to the cider-bearing apple orchards. This custom was most prevalent in the West Country and particularly Somerset—the cider drinking county of the country. Before 1752, the UK's dates were dictated by the Julian Calendar, however, this was changed to a Georgian calendar to bring us in line with the sun's movement around the earth. These changes removed 11 days from the year, however, many people continued to carry out certain customs by the old calendar, therefore, the 17th of January was the most common date for locals to go out and bless the trees.

The custom of giving thanks to the trees for a bountiful harvest is believed to stem from the pagan tradition, which, as well as giving thanks, would also frighten away any evil spirits. The custom would normally begin around 7 pm. A bonfire would be lit in the orchard and a wooden goblet of hot spiced cider, bobbing with roasted apples, small pieces of toast, and spices, was normally provided by the owner of the orchard. The revellers would gather around the oldest tree in the orchard, which was believed to be providing fertility to the younger ones, and a circle formed. The appointed Queen of the wassail was placed into the boughs of the tree to make a toast, people would sing and dance, banging on drums and making merriment.

Together, they would sing:

'Old Apple Tree, I wassail thee,
And Well Mayst thou Bear,
Hat full, cup full, rooms full,
For cider bright and fair'

Cider was then sprinkled around the roots and thrown up into the tree to offer thanks and to promote a bountiful harvest in the following year. The soggy toast would be placed in between the roots as an offering to the robins. Once the Queen was back on the ground, the men would fire shots up through the branches of the tree to frighten away evil spirits. At the height of this custom, this merriment and cider-drinking could continue into the night with all local orchards being visited and thanked.

Although wassailing was a common custom to celebrate the festive period, there were occasions where the proceedings resulted in violent drunkenness. In January 1877, George Gill of Bishops Hull, near Taunton, was charged by Reverend Walter of assault. Whilst out getting merry, a group of men wassailing in the area, knocked on the door of the reverend asking for donations to their celebration. The reverend, finding the men quite drunk, refused to give any money, and asked them to leave, telling them he did not engage with inebriated people. George Gill took great offence to this accusation and struck the reverend several times in the face, knocking him to the ground and taking his candlestick from him. The reverend, sporting a black eye and bleeding nose, got back to his feet and ordered the candlestick to be returned, to which Gill replied he would only give it back if he paid him one shilling. The reverend refused and the men took the candlestick away. George Gill was sentenced to one month of hard labour and a seven shilling fine.

The custom of wassailing is still carried out in parts of Somerset. In Curry Rivel, the celebration takes place along with the burning of the ashen faggot on the 5th of January, whilst Carhampton celebrates using the pre-1752 date of the 17th January.

Reeve's Feast

In the village of North Curry, there was a unique custom with which its origins are disputed. The village would follow a ritual every Boxing Day, which involved feasting on local produce and drinking copious amounts of alcohol until two candles burnt out. Some say this custom originated in the 12th century and the reign of King John. Although John was not the most popular or accomplished monarch, the locals of North Curry appeared to be very fond of him. He visited the village at least three times during his reign and granted permission for locals to hold a weekly market. Connections to the king are confirmed by records of the feast taking place and an effigy of the monarch appearing on the large mince pie prepared for the feast. However, North Curry has a detailed Saxon history, and it seems more likely that the reeve's feast dates back to medieval times and was associated with land tenure and the right to pasture animals.

The reeve, also known as a sheriff, was responsible for funding the feast and would levy local landowners for money and resources to lay the annual celebration on. On Christmas Eve, the reeve of the parish would bring three large heifers to the manor's pound to be inspected by locals. If the beasts were not considered satisfactory in size, the reeve would have to replace them. Once approval was met, a local butcher was instructed to slaughter and prepare the animals. Two local tenants, referred to as dealers, would then attend the reeve's home to cut and divide the meat. During their visit, the reeve would provide these men with a hearty breakfast of beef and onions, marrow beans, and marrow on toast. Food was then divided between seven freehold manors. The reeve of West Hatch would then attend the home of the reeve of North Curry to receive half a bullock to share with his own tenants in return for five shillings. Before the West Hatch visitor could enter the house, he was compelled to speak the following rhyme:

'King John he was a noble knight,

I am come to demand my right,

Open the door and let me in,

Else I'll carry away my money again'

The actual feast would always be carried out on the day after Christmas, unless that day was a Sunday, if so, the feast would take place 24 hours later. Two lords were selected from the manor and were called 'Jack of Knapp' and 'Jack of Slough', these names were believed to be of historical lords in the village's history. These men would be accompanied by assistants and would arrive at 1 pm on the day of the feast to the reeve's residence. Once inside, the Jack of Knapp would be given the key to the reeve's cellar and his assistants would fetch at least one hogshead of ale. The feast could then begin. An elaborate table of meats, stews, and bread were laid out. A local female servant would then present a large mince pie to the table—in the centre of the pie there was a pastry-made effigy of King John standing proudly upright. Before eating began, food was taken from the table for the tenants and poor of the parish. Once the men were ready to indulge, two 1lb candles were lit and the two 'Jacks' and their assistants could consume as much food and ale as they wished until the candles extinguished themselves. Once the feast was over, a toast would be raised to King John, the original Jacks, and to the army and navy.

The last feast that took place in its original form was in 1868. Like many other changes that took place in the more moral Victorian era, many felt this celebration was just an excuse for eating and drinking to excess, one vicar claiming the men would just relight the candles to continue their overindulgence. Changes were made to encourage donations to charities rather than debauchery. In July 1890, the Taunton Courier reported that the reeve's feast charity had donated over two hundred blankets to the poor of the parish. The charity also regularly gave out bags of coal, clothing, and food to the less fortunate. Although the feast came to an end in the mid-1860s, the charity is still in effect to this day and holds an annual picnic to celebrate the history of this incredibly unique custom.

The Hobby Horse of Minehead

The Minehead custom of the hobby horse is incredibly unique and of which the origins are unclear. Some suggest it began with an attempt to frighten off the invasion of the Danes in the Anglo-Saxon times, whilst others think it began to commemorate the wreck of a ship. The custom is carried out on the eve of May Day and featured the effigy of a horse made with sack cloths and decorated with bright colours and ribbons. The words 'sailor's horse' painted on the side, the structure was large and quite heavy and resembled the shape of a boat rather than a horse. A man would stand in the middle with his decorated face or wearing a mask for all to see. The hobby horse would weave and dance through the streets of Minehead and Dunster, accompanied by musicians and a large crowd who were singing folk songs merrily and collecting donations from onlookers.

The Luttrells of Dunster Castle had a great fondness for this May Day tradition, and from 1792, the hobby horse and procession were invited to visit the castle. Here they were greeted with ale or cider, food, and monetary contribution. The Queen of May is still crowned at the castle to this day. In the older days of the tradition, the hobby horse was accompanied by assistants who collected donations. Any man unwilling to give over a coin would be lifted by the legs and held upside down, then after a certain amount of drumbeats, the man would be dropped to the ground or beaten with the horse's tail or an old boot. A similar custom is carried out in Padstow in Cornwall and an old local story claims the sailors from the Cornish town stole the Minehead hobby horse and took it home, replicating the tradition. However, others say the Padstow procession is older and grander than ours in Somerset.

Although the hobby horse was a centuries-old custom, by the later 1800s, many in the area felt this parade was a nuisance, demanding money from hard-working locals and allowing people to become rowdy and drunk.

In 1895, the West Somerset Free Press described the procession as 'a recurring nuisance that locals would rather see honoured by its breach than its observance', stating, 'During the day the grotesque figure was the butt of the amusement for the juveniles, but in the evening drew a larger rowdier crowd'.

However much some people may find the custom disruptive, the four day celebration is still carried out in Minehead and greatly enjoyed by the community. On the last night which locals refer to as booty night, the practice of catching willing victims and gentle persuasion for donations is still fondly enjoyed, with the victims dancing with the horse attempting to avoid being whipped by its tail. All donations from the event are given to the Royal National Lifeboat Institution and Mencap.

Egg Shackling

In the South of Somerset, the custom of egg shackling has been celebrated for many years by local children. In the villages of Langport, Martock, Shepton Beauchamp, and Stoke St Gregory, local schools would celebrate Shrove Tuesday with an egg shaking competition. Each child would bring an egg to school with their name written in pencil to give to the teacher, who would then place them in a paper-lined sieve. Each child would give the sieve-filled eggs a good shake and any cracked eggs would then be removed. The last egg remaining crack-free in the sieve would be the winner. The winning child would wear a colourful silk cone-shaped hat which was called the Victor's Cap, and led the children through the parish, collecting money from the locals. Once their tour was complete, they would use the money to buy oranges, nuts, and cakes which were divided between the children. Stoke St Gregory school appears to be the only school in the county that continues to honour this wonderful custom. Egg shackling is celebrated annually at Easter, alongside egg decoration. The children are awarded small prizes for the winners. A source at the school informs me that the century old myths and techniques of how to triumph at egg-shackling continues into modern times.

Punky Night

Punky night is a custom in the villages of Hinton St George and Lopen and is hundreds of years old. It is believed to originate from an occasion in the distant past when local men from both villages attended Chiselborough Fair and did not return. Concerned for their safety, their wives joined together to go and search for them, making lanterns from Mangelweasel, also known as Mangold, a turnip-like vegetable. Every year on the last Thursday in October, children create their own lanterns by hollowing out this vegetable and adding a candle inside, much like the

Halloween tradition of pumpkins. The children will be led through the village, carrying their lanterns by the Punky King and Queen, many dressed up in spooky outfits and all chanting the Punky Night Rhyme:

'Punky Night tonight, Punky Night Tonight

Adam and Eve wouldn't believe

Its punky night tonight, Punky night tonight

Give us a candle, give us a light,

Its Punky night tonight'

The celebration also includes Morris dancing and food and drink. The community then gathers at the village hall where the lanterns are hung from a beam and are judged for creativity with the participants awarded prizes. This custom is still celebrated in Hinton St George every year with recent fundraising paying for new play equipment, parties for the local children, and donations to the village pre-school.

Skimmerton Riding

This custom is not singular to Somerset, but more to the South of England. As a writer, I found the process so intriguing that I had to include it in this book. There is a Skimmerton Lane in the town of Bridgwater and I cannot confirm but would like to think this lane got its name from the public humiliation of this custom. The name Skimmerton derives from the cooking utensil, the Skimmer, which would be used to not only drain liquids from food, but also to make a loud noise and attract attention.

Skimmerton riding or riding the Skimmery was a custom in which local people (normally men) were publicly ridiculed for being unable to control his wife. Some would have come to the attention of the community via gossip and other times the married couple may have aired their dirty laundry in public. The community would come together to bring attention to this family's scandal and immorality in the most public way. The most common reasons for a couple to be subjected to this ordeal were:

- When the man and wife had publicly quarrelled and the male submitted to his wife's behaviour
- The wife was suspected or proven to have been unfaithful and the husband had forgiven her
- Some mistreatments of the husband had been witnessed by the community at the hands of his wife.

At dusk, locals would gather and two people would sit back to back on a horse or donkey, joined by others either in a cart or on foot. The two people on the horse would imitate the victims of the procession, mimicking their arguments or accusations of adultery and carrying effigies of their faces on poles. The procession would move through the village followed by a rowdy rabble who would bang their skimmers and ladles against pans, blow horns, and shout to mock the couple in question.

The procession would then make its way to their victim's house, putting on an elaborate and offensive display outside their home. These displays of the local's disgust could sometimes last as long as nine consecutive nights, with the effigies being burnt on the last night.

It is impossible to determine when or how this custom began but it continued as late as 1900 in some parts of Somerset. Although most Skimmerton rides were performed to shame the act of adultery or to humiliate a hen-pecked husband, sometimes communities also punished those who committed a local crime, or in the case of a man in Milborne Port in 1890, because he had left the windows of the bedroom his children slept in open on a cold winters night! In Kenton Mandeville, a man was ridiculed outside his home for sporting a black eye inflicted by his wife, the story goes that he went outside and challenged any man to come in and try and deal with his wife to which they all cowered away. One of the crowd shouted that she needed a good leathering. The hot-headed woman inside the house heard the comment and came storming towards the crowd with a fire poker, the crowd quickly ran and never bothered the family again. The Skimmerton tradition would also be used to expose a bankrupt or suspected homosexual.

In 1900, a woman named Hedwig Green of Oakhill near Shepton Mallet brought seven men before the magistrate accused of assault. Richard and Hedwig had lived in their house for eight years and had five children, three of which were living. Hedwig had recently had her brother from their native Germany come to stay and this caused much disharmony in an already unhappy marriage. Richard could be violent towards his wife when he'd had a drink and his brother in law was aware of his sister's mistreatment. Complaining to locals at the Oakhill Brewery about the visitor, Richard got an idea in his head that this man was not in fact his wife's brother but her illicit lover. He went to the local vicar to discuss his fears and word had spread in the community.

On the night of the assault, Hedwig was at home with her brother and children, her husband had not yet returned, when she heard loud banging and shouting approaching her home. After locking her brother in the bedroom with the children, she went downstairs to fasten the door, where a gathering of over fifty people began throwing large stones at the house. Refusing to come out, the mob then began breaking down the door, reaching in and dragging the woman six yards into the garden. The mob then continued to throw stones and dirt at her whilst shouting obscene insults and demanding she present the mysterious German man to them. She continued to refuse and withstood the attack until it subsided. All this time, her husband remained out of sight, even though he was aware a 'skimmerton riding' was taking place at his home.

At court, the men denied any physical contact and although confirming they were present, defended their behaviour by stating they were only following an age-old custom when a woman was suspected of adultery. Their solicitor argued that this practice was carried out across the country and these respectable men were only carrying out her husband's wishes.

Although a doctor provided evidence of Mrs Green having been bedridden with shock, bruising, and scratches on the day after the attack, the judge found just one man guilty and fined him two shillings. The Greens left the village shortly after and moved to Bath.

Glatt Hunting

Glatt hunting, otherwise known as hunting the conger eels, was a tradition on Kilve beach for hundreds of years and only really ceased in the 1950s. on the 14th October each year, local men would attend the beach in low tide, dressed in their oldest clothes and brandishing a six-foot-long stick which had been bevelled into the shape of a chisel at one end. Accompanied by their trusty dog, a spaniel was found to be best, the local men would wade through the water, moving rocks to find eels. The dogs were skilled in seeking out the prey, much like rabbit hunting, and would scratch the sand to indicate to his master that something lay beneath. These eels tended to weigh around four pounds, however, some were reported as being over twenty pounds and capable of inflicting quite a nasty bite to the hands of their hunters.

Bull-Baiting

The barbarous act of bull-baiting was held yearly in the marketplace and streets of Axbridge on the anniversary of the gunpowder plot, the 5th of November. Although a medieval custom, also carried out in other parts of England, this was considered one of the most shameful of our county. I will not go into any details about what took place, but it clearly involved the torturing and killing of the animal. The act of bull-baiting, also referred to as bull running, was banned by parliament in 1835, however, Axbridge and Wells both continued with the custom until 1838, many locals had heavy fines implemented which brought the act to a halt.

A Piglet for the Mayoress

In Bridgwater, it was customary that when a new town mayor was elected, his wife, the mayoress, would be gifted with the tenth piglet from the litters of all local farms. This custom seemed to end in the mid-1850s.

Wedding Customs

In Stoke Cursey (Stogursey), as a wedding ceremony took place, locals would place a chain or rope across the church entrance. The wedding party could not pass until they paid the children of the village a fee. There is also an alternative version of this custom in Nether Stowey in which wagons would line the street leading up to the church, blocking the wedding party from passing until they paid a toll.

Handkerchief Mourners

The village of Shipham held its own custom at the burial of a child in the parish. The women mourners would wear their customary black but place a white handkerchief on their heads. Breaking tradition, these women would then carry the coffin to the church. Some say this has some resemblance to the Catholic faith.

Crossing the Bells

In Henstridge, a small village near the Dorset border, on the day of a funeral, the sexton would attend the bells at noon and ring six strokes on each bell, beginning with the treble and working down in tone to the tenor.

Hunting the Hare

In Chard, it was an annual custom to provide a hare for the dinner of the baron. On the morning of the anniversary, a local pack of hounds would hunt the manor grounds. The first hare caught would be sent up to the cook to be baked.

Badger Feast

In Ilchester, a bizarre custom was enjoyed on Christmas Eve with the feasting on a roasted badger. The custom began in Norman times and was carried out in a secret location in the woods by local poachers. In more modern times, young men from the community would catch and skin a badger and take it to the Cow Inn, where it would be roasted over an open fire. Locals would pay for the pleasure of basting the meat and sampling the food which apparently tastes like veal. But no cutlery was allowed, the meat could only be cut with a penknife or pulled with fingers! Ilchester also enjoyed an annual pipe puffing competition in which twelve men would bring their clay pipes and, on the word "Go", try to be the first to smoke his pipe clean. This victorious man would then be known as the champion pipe smoker of Somerset. But beware, if a contestant was caught using any more than two matches to light his pipe, he was immediately disqualified.

S Jenner, Circa 1850 the Welcome Collection

Pork Rationing

In the villages surrounding Chilton Polden on the Mendips, local farmers were in trouble with the authorities during the Second World War for breaking rationing rules to follow a custom. It was customary in this area for a farmer who slaughtered his pig to give a cut to his neighbour, on the understanding that when the receiver slaughtered his own pig, he would return the favour. At least five farmers appeared before the magistrate during the war years for this crime.

Legends

We all love a legend. We may not realise it but we have all grown up with legends, whether it be Father Christmas, the Easter Bunny, or a strange woman down the road who eats children that step foot in her garden. When I was a child, I had an uncle named Howard, known in the family as Cuthbert. Uncle Howard was a Cornish man who had lived in Somerset for many years. He had adopted an amusing mixed-county dialect and having spent his life swede-bashing and drinking copious amounts of proper Somerset cider across the county, he had a story or two to tell. Sadly, he has now passed away, but he filled my childhood with awe. When he wasn't enthralling me with the mystery of how he could remove his teeth when mine just wouldn't budge (dentures, just to be clear), he filled my days with wonderful stories of fairies at the bottom of the garden, highwaymen buried at the local crossroads, and of great black beasts who wandered the moors. 'Oh, you don't believe me then, Gogs?' Gogs was a childhood nickname. 'I'm telling ee', my handsome, fifty times the size of a normal cat he was, chased me and old John all across waascom, he did, teeth like knives, they were, I'm tellin ee'. My father always attributed Uncle Howard's stories to too many pints of Scrumpy, but although ridiculed by the family, he set my imagination in motion. His stories were as integral to my upbringing as the beautiful scenery and local people that I knew while growing up in a small village.

There are hundreds of legends in Somerset, they all variate in their location, origin, meaning, and many have unknown original sources. A legend does not need evidence to support it, these stories are passed down from generation to generation and only a fool would question their authenticity. I have researched many legends to write this chapter and have made a point of steering away from well-known stories such as Alfred and his Cakes or St Dunstan of Glastonbury, and instead, researched more localised and unique legends. I retell these wonderful legends as I have interpreted them. I am sure that some reading this chapter will know a slightly different version or place the legend at a different landmark. Over the centuries, these wonderful stories are passed down and it seems the storyteller, or perhaps the one enjoying the story, can interpret and retell their own understood version.

Giants

The Legends of Giants is a story told across the world and not singular to Somerset. The belief in giants dates back to ancient times. These abnormally tall men are always portrayed as violent human-eating beings who are set out to destroy everything in their path, as portrayed in the bible with David and Goliath. Up until the fine works of Roald Dahl's BFG, there seems to be very few stories with which the giant is portrayed as anything other than a nuisance and a beast to be slayed by a local warrior.

In Somerset, there are many legends associated with giants. In Brent Knoll, there stands a hill fort once known as the mount of frogs. In the 12th century, a chronicler recorded that King Arthur was aware there were three vicious giants living on the mount. At court, he was acquainted with a bold young man named Ider who had the potential to do great things. King Arthur told the man that if he went with the army to slay the three giants he would be knighted. Eager to prove himself and blessed with the arrogance of youth, Ider went ahead of the army and fought the three giants alone. He did manage to slay all three but was gravely injured. By the time King Arthur and his men arrived, the young man had died of his injuries. King Arthur was racked with guilt over sending the young man to complete such an enormous task and gave the land to the abbey, asking the monks to pray for Ider's soul. This is just one of many legends of Somerset Giants, who are often given responsibilities for the natural landscape in the county. Many stones, dips in hills, and landmarks are attributed to giants and their untimely deaths at the end of the slayer.

Joseph Neal Sewell was born in Lincolnshire in 1805, and like many other poor men, travelled around the country looking for work. However, Joseph was different to others as he stood seven feet and four inches tall and weighed thirty-seven stone. At the age of nineteen, he arrived in Swansea, Wales, where he was struck with Typhoid fever, which claimed his eyesight and put him in the poor house. Once recovered from the illness, he left Swansea and moved onto Bristol before eventually arriving in Taunton. When he arrived in his destitute state, prevented from working by his blindness, the people of Taunton took pity on him and raised money to buy him a caravan. He then went on to meet a man named Bromsgrove who owned a travelling show. The man showed Joseph much kindness and offered him an opportunity to earn a living by amazing the show's visitors with his great height and stature.

The travelling show toured all around the country, and when it arrived at Swansea, Joseph again fell gravely ill. Bromsgrove offered him tea and rest, but the giant began fitting in the afternoon and had died by the evening at the age of 24. In his lifetime, Joseph had been aware of the public's fascination with his height and made Bromsgrove promise that, in death, his remains would not fall into the hands of the anatomists. Although he was offered a great deal of money, the showman kept his promise and returned Joseph to Taunton where he was laid to rest at St Mary's Church. The funeral was attended by many local people who were very fond of their beloved giant. One of the attendees was a man named Farnham, a well-known Somerset dwarf and dear friend to Joseph.

Fairies

The South West of England has many legends of fairies. The counties of Cornwall, Devon, and Somerset all have stories of fairies, pixies, and sprites which lived among the forests. Whilst the Cornwall fairies are always described as quite pesky, the Somerset legends tend to be kinder and more well-behaved. There are legends of punishments dished out by these little beings if a person were to disrupt their homes or attempt to converse with them. The areas of Exmoor and the Quantocks were the locations of many sightings and stories of fairies and pixies. In the village of Stolford, there is a story of a ploughman who, whilst on his travels, came across a tiny baker's bread shovel on the ground, which had been snapped in half. The man repaired the tiny implement before continuing on his way. On his return, the man revisited the spot to find that the shovel was gone, and in its place, was a lovely cake.

Another farmer in the same area told locals that whilst working in his yard one afternoon, he heard the sound of threshing coming from his barn. Knowing he had no labourers on site, he peeped into the barn to see hundreds of red capped pixies working his corn. Astounded by the sight and grateful for the help, the farmer said, 'Well done, my little fellows.' As he spoke, he frightened the pixies, who quickly ran away, never to return. The village of Selworthy had many stories of helpful pixies who would climb through the keyhole at night to clean messy homes, help brew beer, and repair clothes. In return, the household would leave a bowl of milk and bread in the corner of the room whilst some left clean water and towels to allow their little visitors to bathe. As late as 1897, stories of fairies came from the village. Many said they had witnessed tiny fairy fires, and on one occasion, a lady returning home on a summers afternoon in a coach claimed to see little colourful people, who she first thought were children dancing across the road. Warning her driver to be careful, he too confirmed the sighting. But as the coach approached, the dancing fairies vanished.

In Exmoor, farmers believed the pixies and fairies to be helpful around harvest time and would take meats and drinks out to the field, and when they returned the following morning, the goods would be gone and a substantial amount of work carried out. There have also been many fairy legends away from

Exmoor and The Quantocks. In Nempnett Thrubwell in North East Somerset sits the Fairy Toot, an oval barrow which was once a burial chamber. Many locals believed they could hear singing from under the ground and saw little people waving from the grass. Local women would bring their poorly children there in the hope of the fairies healing powers.

Fairy Gifts J A Fitzgerald 1868

Fairy fair – Coombe St Nicholas

A long time ago, a story was told in Combe St Nicholas, near Chard, of a man who once spotted a strange gathering on the hills on his way home. Looking over Blagdon Hill, he could see little people dressed in colourful outfits and high crowned hats enjoying a summer fair. The man witnessed dancing, music, and stalls selling the wares and refreshments normally seen at a village fair. Knowing for certain there were no local fairs advertised in the area, he rode slowly and carefully towards the merriment to investigate. As he rode closer, the music and gaiety continued, but once he arrived on the spot, the whole celebration had completely vanished. Puzzled, he moved around the site but could find no evidence of what he saw from afar. His curiosity was then curbed as he was struck with a violent pain in his side, so he decided to go home. As he rode away, the fair and the music appeared once more, but the man was so stricken with pain that he continued on home. From that day, the man was afflicted with a pain in his side for the rest of his days. Locals of Combe St Nicholas, who told this story in the early 1800s, and families of varying social status confirmed they had witnessed the fair on their travels to and fro to Taunton market, but knowing the fate of the incapacitated man, they refrained from attempting to go anywhere near the celebration.

Luscombe's Race – Northmoor Green

Not all fairies and pixies were known for their kindness. Mischievous fairies were known to avenge local human's bad behaviour or for disturbing their home. There is a common legend that if a person were to disturb a fairy celebration during the late hours, they may be pixie-led. The pixie or fairy would offer to help the human through the dark night back to safety but would instead lead them across the woods and moors for hours. The human unable to break the spell, would follow in a trance -like state until the pixie tired of his amusement.

At an undated time, a wise woman named Molly Green lived on the cold secluded area of Northmoor Green near North Petherton. Molly was held in high esteem in her community for her wisdom, healing powers, and fortune-telling. Molly once told the story of Farmer Luscombe and his wicked ways. Farmer Luscombe was a formidable man, fearful of no man or beast. He was well known for his violent temper and bitter disposition. On a frosty winter evening, the night sky clear of clouds, with bright stars and a full moon, Farmer Luscombe took a walk to check his cattle. Armed with a stick and a whip, he would take walks, on the lookout for wild dogs and trespassers. As he wandered across his land, he struck the ground with his whip, disturbing some ravens from their nest. As they crossed his path, he struck out with his stick, striking one of the birds on the back. Whilst he stood and chuckled at his cruel act, the ground before him suddenly moved and a dwarf-like creature appeared before him. The creature spoke with the sound of a crow's cry:

'Stop sturdy farmer, stop there.

Tis upon fairy ground you be

We hold our court tonight, and soon

Will play pranks before the full moon.'

The dwarf then struck the farmer in the legs, bringing him to the ground with a thump. Whilst Luscombe tried and failed to get back on his feet, he witnessed a crowd of fairies coming up from the ground. 'A race, a race, a race!' they exclaimed as they magically summoned many wild colts, to which they climbed on their backs. The dwarf ordered Farmer Luscombe to mount a horse and they set off, racing through the fields at a thunderous speed, the fairies shrieking and shouting in enjoyment. The race went on for over an hour and the farmer travelled at an unnatural speed, petrified as he was thrown around amongst the racing creatures. Once the races were complete, the fairies picked up the dwarf and threw him around like the hero and leader they clearly considered him to be. The sound of a tinkling bell brought the revelry to an abrupt end and the dwarf, fairies, and colts magically vanished.

Farmer Luscombe was found the following morning, laying in a heap in a field. He was in a stupor and unable to explain to anyone what he had experienced. He laid in bed for a week until he was recovered to return to his normal life. The farmer became a new man, he was no longer quick-tempered and argumentative, but instead, practiced only good deeds and spoke only kind words. Hearing the farmer's account and astounded at the changed man, no local person ever dared strike the ground on Northmoor Green on a full moon.

Dragons

The belief in dragons in the western world began in the middle ages with the Anglo-Saxon superstition regarding death and fire. These winged fire-breathing serpents were said to terrorise communities, sometimes protecting treasure but always wreaking havoc and burning down villages. In Somerset, there are many dragon legends. All of which depict a heroic member of the community slaying the creature and becoming a local hero. The dragon of Aller is one of the most well-known legends which dates back to the 15th century and has been told in different ways over the centuries of storytelling. The first account tells that a flying serpent lived among the hills overlooking the village of Aller. The creature would fly from hill to hill, placing poison down as it went. The dragon struck fear into the villagers, swooping down to steal milk from unsuspecting milkmaids. A local man named John Aller decided the community needed to be free of this pest, and so, covering himself in pitch, wearing a mask and carrying a spear, the brave man went to the dragon's lair and successfully killed the dragon. After his brave act, he was a local hero, and after his death, an effigy was placed in the church. Variations of this story state that he died whilst assassinating the creature, whilst others say he lived on.

An alternative legend for the Aller dragon involved a man name Sir Reginald. Witnessing the devastation the dragon was causing as it swooped down and consumed locals like a snack, he waited until he saw it leave its lair, crept up the hill, and killed three baby dragons. He then fortified the entrance so that when the dragon returned home, stuffed after munching on a local woman, he fought the dragon bravely, eventually slaying it. As the dragon died, he fell heavily, causing a hole in the hillside.

The legend of the Norton Fitzwarren dragon is said to have dated back a thousand years and was described as a scaley spiteful dragon that protected a large collection of treasure. He too struck fear into the hearts of the country-folk but was well-behaved until a local man found his treasure and stole a gold goblet. As the dragon realised it was missing, a great rage was unleashed, and when the night struck, he carried out a devastating attack, burning homesteads to the ground whilst searching for his treasure.

Not one home stood intact that night and many lives were lost. As the dragon returned home to sleep, a local man referred to as Lord of the Storm-Folk was furious with the damage caused and life's taken and swore revenge.

Friedich Justin Bertich 1806

A great battle then commenced between them of which the Lord struck the dragon many times before administering a fatal blow to the dragon's body, cutting him right down the middle. As the dragon fell, the lord himself collapsed, having suffered many wounds. Muttering, 'I cannot be any longer here,' he died on the hillside.

On the Quantocks in the ancient Shervage Wood, there long lives the legend of Gurt Worm—Germanic spelling of great dragon. The legend tells that there was once a huge dragon, the size of three great oak trees, who caused a nuisance in the area, eating cattle and destroying crops. One day, a woodcutter from the village of Stogumber ventured into the wood and stopped on what he thought was a log to have his lunch of bread and cheese. The log then began to move and the man, realising this was the infamous dragon, sliced his knife through the creature, cutting it in half. One half flying over to Billbrook, near Minehead, and the other to Kingston St Mary, a village near Taunton. This story is depicted in the church of Crowcombe on the end of a pew.

On the 23rd October 1766 Mr F C Thomas reported the sighting of a dragon flying over the city of Bath, the local newspaper reported his sighting to the local area. Described as 'the body of that a man but of the blackest of colour. A head like a serpent with a forked tongue, from which from it came a foam so poisonous that whoever it dropped on were sure to perish. The legs were exceptionally long, the feet cloven like that of a devil. It had a thousand wings and his tail divided like a cat and nine tails'. He claimed to witness the beast whip down three women. After describing the dragon the author went on to warn all local people to arm themselves in case the creature returned, adding that any man who was brave enough to tackle the dragon would be esteemed as the second saint George of England. No further sightings were reported.

Drakes Ball – Combe Sydenham, Stogumber

In the beautiful village of Stogumber, there is a legend that involves a beautiful manor house and a 16th century love story. Elizabeth Sydenham was the only surviving daughter of the high sheriff of Somerset, and around the age of thirty was promised to Sir Francis Drake, renowned sea captain explorer and widow. The couple were very much in love despite their twenty-year age gap. As Drake was embarking on a lengthy voyage, he begged Elizabeth to wait for him, saying, 'Be true, dear Bess, I may be away for some years but I will send you a token that I am alive and well.'

Many years passed and Elizabeth heard nothing from her love and it was assumed he had died at sea. Being pressed by her father to marry, she agreed to forget Drake and to settle with an eager suitor. On the morning of her wedding, as she stepped from her home at Combe Sydenham, a large cannonball weighing a hundred pounds fell through the sky at her feet. Announcing this was a token from Francis, fired from hundreds of miles away, Elizabeth cancelled her nuptials and waited for her love to return. Sir Francis Drake and Elizabeth Sydenham married on 25th August 1595 at Stogumber church. This legend has an alternative account which was that Elizabeth was stood at the altar of the church when the ball fell through the roof of the church and landed at her feet,

Sir Francis Drake - Marcus Gheeraerts 1590

accompanied by a fierce storm, and that the ball was actually a meteorite. The mysterious heavy ball is now displayed at the Museum of Somerset, but legend says if ever removed from Combe Sydenham, it always finds its way back home.

Pocock of Chilton Polden

Pocock was an infamous highwayman said to have ridden the roads between Bridgwater and Street in the 16th Century. The legendary Pocock is believed to have lived in a cave near to Chilton Priory, in the village of Chilton Polden. Relying on the Chilton Hills solely as his home, his cave had three caverns inside where he lived, slept, and kept his horse. His horse allegedly wore unusual horseshoes designed by Pocock to enable him to escape capture. Living in a cave with no provisions, Pocock was known for having hair, beard, and nails which were never cut, and he never washed. These living habits may have made the man rather unpopular but, in fact, he was much loved in the community for his kindness to the poor.

The formidable highwayman who roamed the area looking for wealthy travellers never robbed women and children, instead he would offer help and food to those he found lost in Loxley Woods. Pocock was said to have passed on his spoils of plunder to the local poor, which made him more annoying to the local lawmakers. It is unclear how long Pocock evaded capture, but finally, he was discovered in his cave. He fought gallantly for his freedom but was taken, bleeding and battered, to the hangman where he was executed. In the years following his death, Pocock was a celebrated hero in the area with locals singing a song whilst bringing in the harvest:

Rynne, mye bones, ryne the moon shines bright,
Pocock in his cave, his presence is lyte.
But when the night is mirky and darke
He's off on his steed, blythe as a larke.'

Over the years, many travellers have reported paranormal activity on the stretch of road between Ashcott and Bridgwater, one of which claimed she could see a man on horseback who, whilst seeming to be in full gallop, was stuck in place, and another stating an apparition appeared at the side of the road pointing into the distance.

The Screaming Skull of Chilton Cantelo

In St James' Church, in the small village of Chilton Cantelo, just a few miles from Yeovil, rests a man named Theophilus Brome. His inscription reads:

'Here lyeth the body of Theophilus Brome, of the Bromes, of the house of Woodlowes near Warwick Towne in the county of Warwick, deceased 18th August 1870 aged 69, a man just in the actions of his life, true to his friends, forgave those who wronged him, and dyed in peace'

Local legend tells the story of Theophilus's life during the civil war, in which the life-long royalist changed his political stance when he witnessed the King's men's treatment of their prisoners. Theophilus remained in the village once the war was over and Charles II was restored to the throne, living with his sister at Higher Chilton Farm. The man feared the King's retribution would come to him at his death with fears that his head would be removed and given to the monarch on a stake. He implored his sister to promise that at his death, his head would be removed and kept in their home which she agreed. When he died in 1670, his sister kept her promise. His head was removed and placed in a box at the house, sitting above a doorway in the hall. Once his sister also passed, new tenants came, and not relishing the thought of a skull in their home, they attempted to have the skull buried.

When the skull was removed, a terrible scream and poltergeist activity engulfed the house which could not be stopped, so the skull was returned to the box. In 1770, a church sexton attempted once more to bury the head in the churchyard, and again, a deaf-defying scream tortured the house and the spade he used to dig snapped in half. During restoration work at St James' church, Theophilus's tomb was opened and his corpse confirmed his head had indeed been removed. Since then, no one has attempted to remove the skull from the house.

The Hounds of Langford Budville

Many years ago, a very callous and mean-spirited man lived in the village of Langford Budville. This squire kept vicious hounds and took great enjoyment in hunting down animals and watching his hounds destroy them. When intoxicated, his evil pleasures only worsened. On New Year's Eve, the man and his hounds were out hunting all day, and after, went to a friend's house in the nearby village of Chipley to attend a lavish celebration. Just before midnight, having consumed a large amount of alcohol, the man decided he wanted to return home, but his friends advised against it, stating it was too dangerous with highwaymen lurking and treacherous dark lanes which may damage his horse. Refusing the offer of a bed for the night, the arrogant man told them he didn't care if he met with the devil himself, he would not be concerned if his horse broke its neck, he would do as he pleased and it pleased him to return home.

As the man left the gates of the property, two of his hounds that were lurking about startled his horse. He cursed angrily at the dogs, telling them to go to hell before galloping away, leaving them behind. The man rode furiously through the village, cursing and shouting while his horse attempted to navigate the dark country lanes. As the horse came down a hill where some fir trees stood, it fell to the ground and broke its neck. Tumbling from the horse, the man also suffered a broken neck. Both were found the following morning.

The two hounds now appear every New Year's Eve, just before midnight, with red glowing eyes and lolling tongues, searching for their master. They appear from Young Oaks Woods and run savagely across the common. All through the night, the hounds run up and down the road between French Nut Tree and Carriers Lane, accompanied by the sound of galloping hoofs, shouting, and cursing. Legend states the hounds will never rest until their master returns home.

Swaine's Leap – Loxley Woods

On the A38 between Bridgwater and Ashcott sits the ancient forest known as Loxley Woods. If a visitor walks down through the public footpath, they will notice a signpost for Swaine's Leap. This is four stones placed just a stride from each other which have now been sadly lost in the undergrowth. There are two legends attached to these stones, both set in the aftermath of the Battle of Sedgemoor. The first legend states that rebel prisoners were being led across the Polden Hills by the king's soldiers when they stopped for a rest in the woods. The soldiers began discussing their triumphant battle but could not agree on the width of the Sedgemoor rhine, which had separated the soldiers from the rebels. Two of the soldiers became quite quarrelsome and even the prisoners joined in the debate. One soldier boldly claimed he could jump the width of the rhine with ease, his claim was challenged as the soldiers laid out markers on the ground. Amongst the prisoners was 'giant' Jack Swaine, he was known locally as a giant due to his great height and stature. When he viewed the jumps, he laughed, stating that he could jump much further with ease. The soldiers ridiculed his claim and Swaine offered to prove it.

The soldiers set the large man free temporarily and lined up to disprove the prisoner's claim. Two men stood at the far end with markers at the ready. Jack stepped a few paces and then ran at great speed into a miraculous leap which left everyone in awe. When he landed though, he did not stop but leapt again and again, landing four times before knocking two soldiers to the ground. The men took a hefty fall to the ground, and in the commotion Jack Swaine made his escape, easily navigating the woods he knew so well.

An alternative legend states that there was a man named Jan Swayne who lived at the bottom of a hill near the village of Moorlinch. Jan had supported the Duke of Monmouth's claim to the throne and once the battle was lost, was dragged from his bed to face the judge. Whilst being taken to Bridgwater for trial, he begged the soldiers to untie him so he could say one last goodbye to his children. The soldiers agreed, and once unfastened, Jan took four miraculous leaps in the marshy Loxley Woods where he hid and remained undetected.

Castle Neroche Hillfort

Castle Neroche (known as Castle Racche by locals) is situated near the village of Buckland St Mary, on the Blackdown Hills, nine miles from Chard. The hillfort is believed to be over 2,500 years old and offers beautiful views of the Quantocks and Exmoor. Legend says that a great value of treasure is buried under this fort and that any man who attempts to dig it up will be struck down by the devil. In 1854, Reverend Francis Warre of Hestercombe House wrote that hundreds of years ago, labouring men in the area came to the hillfort to find the treasure. Whilst digging, the men came over with a dreaded fear and abandoned their search. In the following months, all these men succumbed to death, either by accident or illness. Another local story says that the hillfort was always guarded by the devil himself. When brave men of the village of Corfe came to search for the treasure, bringing a clergyman and holy water with them for protection, they found treasure and were overjoyed. But this was short-lived as the chest of treasure sank back down into the ground before their eyes. The devil rose and all men, including the clergyman, were dead within a year.

Jack the Treacle eater – Yeovil

In Barwick Park in Yeovil there sits four follies believed to date back to the 1770s. Jack the treacle eater sits on the eastern side of the estate and is a pretty folly made of a circular tower made of rough rubble, and topped with the vane of a winged young man. Local legend states that Jack was once a messenger boy for the Messiter family. Jack frequently took messages from Yeovil

to London and ate treacle to maintain his stamina. Legend states If a pot of treacle is left by the folly at night, Jack will come down and eat it.

Stanton Drew Stone Circles

In the picturesque village of Stanton Drew, in North Somerset, stands the mysterious stone circles. Larger than their Stonehenge cousins but much less known, the area consists of three stone circles which vary in size. The area has never been excavated but it is believed to date back to 3000BC and the Neolithic period. The first and largest circle, known as the great circle, has a width of 370 feet and consists of twenty-six large stones, though it's believed that many more were once there and that this was actually part of a great structure that once stood here. This area surrounding the circle was believed to have been a ditch, dug seven metres wide with evidence of a large entrance on the north-east side which led to the second smaller stone circle. Although the north-east circle is smaller in diameter, the stones here are the largest of the whole area. Within these stones, there is evidence of large wooden posts and it is suggested to have been the stage of a ritual ceremony. The third circle is on the south-west of the largest and further away from the other circles. Running alongside the stone are two Stoned Avenues which run down to the river Chew. In the gardens of the nearby village pub stand the Cove, three large stones placed near to each other, which are believed to have been the location of ceremonial rituals. These stones are believed to have been sourced from the Mendips Hills and are considered to be older than the circles.

The mystery of these stones has intrigued people for thousands of years and where a definitive explanation cannot be found, the stones have prompted legends, passed down by the generations. The most popular legend of the stones is that a devil's curse turned a merry wedding party to stone on a dawn morning.

Stranton Drewe – Lithograph by William Stukeley

The story goes that a wedding took place on Saturday and the merriment of the celebrations continued into the evening. The party's violinist refused to play after midnight as it was an insult to the church, so the musician was replaced by a mysterious hooded dark man who played his violin into the early hours of Sunday morning, whilst maids danced and men played their fiddles. As the sun came up on the holy day of Sunday, the violin player revealed himself as the devil and turned the party-goers into stone. The Cove stones were the bride, groom, and clergyman, the stones the dancers and the avenues the fiddlers, all frozen in time.

John Aubrey, accomplished writer, visited the area in 1664 and wrote that it was believed locally that on the 6th night after a full moon, these stones awaken at midnight and walk down to the river Chew for a drink of water. Aubrey also wrote about another stone in proximity to the circles known as Hautevilles Quoits. Local wealthy man, Sir Hautevilles, was said to have thrown this rock from a great distance, however, this legend has also been told that the stone thrower was a giant.

Wimblestone – Shipham

The Wimblestone sits in a field between the villages of Winscombe and Shipham in North Somerset. The stone stands at five-foot-five inches and is believed to have been a boundary marker or the burial place of someone significant in the area's history. Many tales are told of the Wimblestone's powers, some stating that the stone protects buried treasure, and that the stone is impossible to move, with Oxen dying in one farmer's attempt. Other legends say that the Wimblestone comes alive at night, walking through the nearby fields, visiting the water stone in Wrington before returning to its spot at dawn. Farm workers in history have claimed they have seen the stone shuffling along the ground, while others claim to have witnessed the stone dance on the first full moon of the month of May.

Naked Boy's Stone – Brendon Hills

Naked boy's stone is located on the B3224 road between Bishops Lydeard and Wheddon Cross, on the spot where the villages of Old

Cleeve, Treborough, Withiel Florey, and Brompton Regis meet. The stone is believed to be a medieval piece of granite that was used as either a marker for an ancient trackway that led to the river Parrett and the village of Combwich, or a boundary marker between the parishes of Old Cleeve and Brompton Regis. The stone is just over a meter in size and is of a triangular appearance. The local legend of naked boy's stone is that on a full moon, an inebriated man, who had been turned to stone for his drunken ways, wakes up and walks down the river to drink from the spring.

The Cursing Well – Bishops Lydeard

In the village of Bishops Lydeard, there sits a well in the lane near the church. There is a local legend woven into the well's history which states that when this well was being built, the workmen were troubled by frequent visits from the devil and sought advice from a local clergyman. The holy man came to the site and witnessed for himself the appearance of the devil disguised as a man but with a cloven hoof revealing his evilness. The clergyman said, 'In the name of the father, the son, and the holy spirit, why troublist thou me?' To which the devil vanished. The clergyman advised the men to quickly wall the devil into the well and he never  appeared again. The well became known as the cursing well or the devil's whispering well, and locals could go there to whisper to the devil himself and curse those that had vexed them. The position of the well allowed visitors to remain unseen as they asked the devil to strike down those that had offended them.

The Glastonbury Thorn

Also known as the holy thorn, the plant grew on Wearyall Hill and legend told that it would miraculously flower at midnight on Christmas eve (5th Jan, before the Georgian calendar of 1752). It was believed that Joseph of Arimathea, a wealthy merchant, and uncle to Jesus Christ, came to the area to spread the gospel. He attended the hill and stopped to rest, striking his staff into the ground. When he awoke, his staff had grown into the holy thorn. For many years, people gathered here in the hope of seeing the opening of the flowers on Christmas morning. Many shoots were taken from the hawthorn and planted elsewhere. The original plant was destroyed in the civil war as it was considered a relic of superstition, but others do grow in other places in the abbey grounds, at the chalice well and St John's Church. The plant is actually known as Crataegus monogyna and does typically flower twice a year.

The Beast of Brassknocker Hill

In 1979, the woods of Brassknocker Hill near Bath became home to a mysterious beast that has never been explained. Local couple, Ron and Betty Harper, noticed in the July that their beautiful old oak tree had been stripped of its bark. The tooth indentations left in the trunk were much larger than the customary squirrel and could not be explained. Within a month, fifty trees in the area had suffered the same damage and locals noticed that the normal activity of wildlife and small animals had disappeared. At the end of August, a local man who wished to remain anonymous stated that whilst driving down a quiet road to Monkton Combe in the evening, he had witnessed a bear-like creature standing on its hind legs. The creature was around four feet in length and had white circles around its eyes.

In the year that followed, many other local people reported sightings of the beast, with descriptions varying from a lemur, baboon, or monkey. In the summer of 1981, a local police inspector witnessed the creature for himself. He was unable to capture the animal but stated with great confidence that it was a chimpanzee. The creature was never caught and eventually, sightings ceased. A few years later, a new sighting was made in the area, but this time was described as a four-legged beast likened to a stag or a polecat. It was eventually discovered that an Alpaca had escaped from a local home.

Neanderthal Man of Hangley Cleave, Exmoor

In the 1850s, the iron mines of Hangley Cleave on Exmoor were worked by local men who reported a sight they could not explain. The men stated that whilst carrying out their work, they frequently noticed a beast watching them who they described as a large crouching man-like form covered with black matted hair with flat eyes. The creature never came near whilst they worked, but when they arrived for work in the early morning, they frequently found their carts tipped over and their work tools strewn around the area. Although this area is now abandoned, a dog walker reported in 1993 that he experienced a presence in the area which frightened his dogs. He said he could smell a horrible smell similar to that of a wet dog and heard the sound of heavy breathing. He attempted to run away but tripped over, and as he looked back, claimed he saw a seven-foot hairy ape-like man. The creature quickly moved into the woods and the frightened man headed home.

Mrs Leakey of Minehead

Susan Leakey was an elderly widow of 17th Century Minehead in West Somerset. The woman was well-known in the town as a kind and friendly person, and many of her friends commented that it would be a great shame when she passed. She always responded that though kind and caring in life, in her death she would return to haunt them all. Mrs Leakey died in the Autumn of 1634 and was laid to rest at Minehead Churchyard on the 5th of November. True to her word, within a week of her burial, Mrs Leakey began to appear in various locations. Wearing the clothes she wore when she died, she haunted the town, the beach, the quay, and the local fields.

People in the community reported seeing her drifting around her old haunts, but contrary to her earthly kind attributes, as a phantom she was formidable. One doctor told how he had met with Mrs Leakey whilst walking across some fields when returning from a late-night visit to a patient. As they walked, they enjoyed a friendly conversation, and as they approached a stile, the doctor gave the woman a hand to climb over. Walking on, the doctor noticed that whilst the elderly woman was talking, her lips were not moving. Looking closer, he noticed her eyes were void and her eyelids were still. Feeling fearful of this apparition, the doctor attempted to put some distance between them, and as they approached the second stile, he quickly climbed over, this time failing to help the old lady. Mrs Leakey took great offence at his lack of manners and promptly kicked the doctor in his britches, causing him to run away quickly.

Mrs Leakey had at least three children who lived in the local area. Although she was a loving mother during her life, in death, her children were not spared her wrath. Her son Alexander, was a successful mariner who moved cargo back and forth from Minehead to Waterford in Ireland. Mrs Leakey would often frequent the quay, waiting for her son's ships to come into view. Blowing her whistle, she would cause great storms, never taking a life, but causing great damage to the ship and sinking her son's profits to the bottom of the sea. Alexander's business was eventually destroyed, with the man left bankrupt and his family living in poverty. Mrs Leakey frequently haunted Alexander's home with some claiming she was responsible for smothering her own grandchild. Alexander's wife, Elizabeth, frequently saw her mother-in-law when she looked into a looking glass. Eventually, the terrified woman bravely confronted her, asking why she would not rest and leave them in peace. Mrs Leakey told Elizabeth she had a task she needed her to complete which involved the old woman's son-in-law, Bishop John Atherton.

John Atherton was married to Mrs Leakey's daughter, Joan. John had worked in a clerical role in the local church but had then moved over to Ireland where he was appointed bishop by Charles I. John was heavily involved in Irish politics, and with a close relationship to the king, was pivotal in reasserting the church's power in Ireland. It seems that Mrs Leakey knew things about her son-in-law that brought his pious image into question. She ordered Elizabeth Leakey to go to Ireland and pass a letter to John Atherton. Although the note was never seen, it was believed that Mrs Leakey told him she knew he had had an affair with her other daughter Susan, (in these times, sex with a sister-in-law would be considered as incest), and that a baby that came from that illicit affair had been murdered by him. She warned him to mend his deceitful and treacherous ways before the king was made aware. Rumours of these accusations soon came to the attention of the king. Charles I ordered three members of his privy council to attend West Somerset and investigate claims of this elderly phantom, her tyranny over the town, and to look for any truth in the rumours about the conduct of his trusted bishop. Although the investigation led to many local people coming forward to share their ghostly encounters, the enquiry found no real evidence of truth in the tales of the whistling ghost or in any wrongdoing by the bishop, the learned men believing this was instead an attempt of blackmail by the bishop's wife's family, who were facing financial ruin. Bishop Atherton kept his job. Not happy with this outcome, Elizabeth Leakey travelled to Ireland, as promised to her ghostly mother-in-law, to deliver the note. Rumours of the bishop's wrongdoing continued to grow. Bishop Atherton's career unravelled, an accusation of sodomy with his male servant, John Goode, sealed his fate and he was hanged in December 1640, his alleged lover executed a few weeks later.

Whether John Atherton's demise was the act of his vindictive ghostly mother-in-law, or if his sister-in-law, Elizabeth Leakey, planned and failed to blackmail the man, Mrs Leakey's legend lives on in Minehead, with many local people still attributing bad weather and choppy waters to the old woman.

Lady Wyndham of Orchard Wyndham

In 1599, legend tells that after a short illness, Lady Florence Wyndham of Orchard Wyndham died and was laid to rest in the family vault at St Decuman's Church in Watchet. The sexton of the church, Tom Hole, knowing that the lady had been buried in her fine clothes and jewellery, waited until the night and returned to the crypt to steal the rings from her fingers. Unable to pull them off, the treacherous sexton sliced the lady's finger off. The corpse suddenly moved, and Lady Wyndham arose from what appeared to have been a trance. Frightened and exposed as a grave robber, the sexton fled the scene, leaving his lantern behind. Lady Wyndham took it to guide her home to her astonished family. She went on to have her only son and bloodline which continued the Wyndham Dynasty to modern times. After Florence's mysterious resurrection, the Wyndham family adopted a new custom that all members of the family would only be buried after three days of death, which is still practised in modern times.

Lucote of Porlock

Porlock is a small coastal village just five miles from Minehead. With a mention in the Domesday Book, Porlock is a beautiful old fishing village. Legend has it that the village was once afflicted by a troublesome local spirit. The undated story tells that the village once had a brutish bully named Lucote who made locals lifes a misery with his arrogance and rudeness. When Lucote died, the village rejoiced and hastily buried him in the local churchyard with no mourners. However, one week after his funeral, the man returned to the village in spirit form, hanging around the church and reinstating his tyranny over the village. Eleven local pastors came together and agreed that an exorcism was needed to rid the village of this brutish phantom. The holy men gathered at the church, and although the exorcism was carried out carefully, the spirit remained jeering and laughing at the men's failure to remove him.

The pastors sought advice from the parson of nearby St Decuman's Church, who agreed to come to Porlock and join them in another attempt to remove the man. The second exorcism was as unsuccessful as the first, and again, Lucote sneered and ridiculed the twelve men. Feeling exasperated, the St Decuman's parson gave Lucote some harsh words, telling him he was a bully and was not wanted anywhere on God's green earth. Lucite was taken aback, no person was ever brave enough to challenge him, the priest noticing a change in the brute continued to taunt him, saying that he may be twice the size of him but he could do so much more. The parson produced a biscuit from underneath his cloak and said, 'I warrant that you cannot chew this biscuit as well as I can'. Lucote laughed heartily at the parson's foolish words, replying, 'If you cannot prove your words, I will tear you limb from limb. But if you are right and I cannot eat it, I will submit and vanish forever'.

The parson brought the biscuit from under his cloak and took a bite, chewing carefully before swallowing. He held the biscuit out to Lucote, who snatched it from him and took a large bite. Immediately, Lucote began to groan in pain, and spitting out the food, he fell shakily to the ground. Realising he had been duped into taking a bite from the holy wafer, Lucote conceded and laid silent, all malice leaving his body. The parson summoned the man outside and told him they would be taking a journey by horse. Together, the men rode through the night, passed Minehead and Watchet and onto the beach at Doniford.

Dismounting by some rocks, the parson produced a small tin box, he placed it down and opened it, ordering Lucote to step inside. The man, all malice and wickedness gone, did as he was ordered, and as he stepped in, he began to shrink smaller and smaller until he could fit perfectly inside. The parson quickly snapped the lid of the box closed and hurled it into the sea where it was carried away by the tide. Lucote was banished to the farthest corner of the world, unable to return for a thousand years.

Superstitions

The dictionary's definition of superstition is 'A widely held but irrational belief in supernatural influences, especially leading to good or bad luck, or a practice based on such a belief'. The belief that a specific event or behaviour can determine an outcome and that this was in the hands of some supernatural influence. We may scoff, but we now have science and education which offers an explanation into most occurrences, but superstition has existed since the earliest times as people tried to understand events that they could not control, such as earthquakes, droughts, and diseases. To believe that a performed ritual could create the desired outcome was a way for humans to try and exercise some control over their fate, where there were suffering and uncertainty. Superstitions were prevalent at a time where explanations were not yet found for outside forces that were unpredictable and damaging to life. The bible itself could be considered to preach superstitious beliefs to those who do not follow the church.

Superstitions present themselves in many forms, including witchcraft, charms, carrying out rituals, avoiding certain creatures or places, lunar phases, and bad omens. Although there are many that are shared across humanity, there are also some that are more prevalent or solely exist in the county of Somerset. I have searched many resources to attempt to gather the superstitions that were, or are, held in the county. There are examples of widely believed superstitions which have influenced the lives of the people of Somerset. The belief in witchcraft, spells and curses were as common in Somerset as anywhere in the world. The misfortune of bad harvests and diseased cattle were commonly met with the suspicions of someone, usually a woman, in the local area casting her evil eye over a person, his family and their livelihood.

The belief in bewitching and 'overlooking' was deep-rooted in Somerset, and through my research, I have found it especially common in the Langport area. Illnesses such as epilepsy or phthisis (tuberculous) were generally attributed to someone who wished you ill-luck. This evil wisher could bewitch their victim by staring directly into his face, into his property or by touch. It was a common belief that people who had a squint were able to cast this terrible spell. If you were to pass a person with a squinty eye, you should spit on the floor to protect yourself. Why would this person want to bestow such bad luck on another? Because they were evil, and that evil had been carried through their forefathers. Jealousy and envy or a simple quarrel could lead a person to inflict great misfortune on a neighbour. Throughout the world, it was common practice to wear charms on necklaces to keep the evil eye away. Horseshoes and the church gargoyles were also believed to offer protection from this phenomenon.

Over the 1800s there are many accounts of families who claimed to have been 'overlooked' by the evil eye in Somerset. In Langport, there was an undated story shared with me about two brothers, one a farmer and one a sawyer. The farmer's wife was struck down with a mystery illness and took to her bed, and at the same time, the farmer's cows were suffering from an unexplained ailment and one cow died of inflammation. As the farmer was burying the carcass, a woman, known locally as the witch of Somerton, passed by and he asked her why he was being struck with such misfortune. The woman replied that his family had been overlooked by some evil wisher, she advised that this bad luck would continue if he did not remove the evil eye that had been cast on his family. She told him that if he crossed her palm with silver, she could attempt to rid him of the curse. The farmer gave her seven shillings and the woman left, promising to start right away. The following day, she returned and mixed a concoction of red powder and egg yolk in the farmer's property. Once blended, she burnt the mixture while muttering words that the farmer and his wife could not understand. She gave the wife the heart of a small animal on a chain and told her to wear it at all times. The farmer gave her another shilling and several eggs to take home to continue her work. The thought of this terrible curse upon his household caused the farmer to become delirious with anxiety, needing to be accompanied at all times to protect him from himself. The farmer's brother, hearing about the declining health of his sibling, came to the village. Once told of his brother suspicions, he also became convinced that he too was being overlooked, accusing their elderly mother who lived locally. The farmer eventually recovered from his hysteria, but sadly, his brother became so unhinged in his accusations of his mother that he had to be confined at the Wells asylum for her safety.

Another South Somerset story, which is again undated, is of a mother of a large family who, over the course of two years, was marred with terrible misfortune. Her husband had developed a chronic illness and two of her children had been severely injured in separate accidents. Feeling exhausted and no doubt browbeaten by her bad luck, she began to suspect that she had been given the evil eye from someone in the community and was being overlooked. She sought advice from a wise man in Wells who confirmed she was cursed and asked her to list the names of local women who may wish her harm. At first, she could not think of anyone but finally came up with a name, to which the man agreed was the culprit. He advised her that much prayer was needed to remove the curse and sent her home with specific instructions. That night, just before, she and her husband knelt before their fire and burnt salt as instructed. They uttered no words for the next hour other than the following chant:

'This is not the thing I wish to burn,
But Mrs _ 's heart of _ Somerset to turn,
Wishing thee neither to eat, drink, sleep, or rest,
Until thou dost come to me and my request
Or else the wrath of god may fall on thee,
And cause thee to be consumed in a moment,
Amen.'

Once the hour of prayer was complete, the couple then took to the staircase, walking up backwards, and repeating the lord's prayer as they went. No other words were spoken until both were in bed. There is no record of whether a woman in the village came forward to confess the curse or whether the family had an improvement of fortunes.

In the North of Somerset, it was customary to remove or protect a family home from the evil eye by taking the heart of a bullock or pig and covering it with pins. If a family suspected they were being overlooked, then the heart should be burnt in the fire, whereas if the pinned heart was more of a precaution or if cattle had mysteriously died, then the heart should be placed up inside the chimney. In 1912, an example of this superstition was found by men renovating a manor house in Marston Magna, who found a charred bullock's heart covered in pins hidden in the crevice of the chimney.

As the 1800s progressed, education and understanding of the world around us grew, and the superstition of the evil eye and curses became ridiculed by many. However, even into the 1900s, rural areas still believed that an enemy could exercise this power over another's fate. In 1929, Mr George Sheppard of Langport appeared before the magistrate charged with making threats towards local man Reuben Lock. Lock told the court that Mr Sheppard had adopted the belief that he had placed the evil eye over him and his wife and had subjected Mr Lock to shouting accusations at him in the street and building monuments in his tree to repel him. Mr Lock told the magistrate that on one occasion, he had asked George Sheppard who he was cussing at, to which he replied, 'You and your hag-riding old wife'. When George Sheppard, who was in his seventies, and his wife spoke to the judge, they repeated their suspicions that Lock had cursed them and attributed their misfortune to his evil doing. The judge stated his disbelief that such a superstition would continue and bound Mr Sheppard over to keep the peace for six months. Hag riding was a term in which people believed that nightmares were caused by witchcraft.

To be hag-ridden meant that a local witch had come into your bedroom at night and sat on your chest while you slept, causing you to have terrifying nightmares. In the 1600s there were men who made a device with a flat board with sharp nails protruding. They would lay this board on their chest before sleeping to prevent an evil woman from hag riding them while they slept.

Along with white witches, curses and wise men, there was also a prophet in the Minehead area known as 'Mother Shipton'. This woman offered the locals many words of wisdom and predictions of things to come, she was held in high esteem by the local labouring villagers and many sought her guidance. One such prophecy hit the national headlines in April 1879 when she

Ham Hill Quarry- credit Ham Hill Historical page Facebook

foretold that at noon on Good Friday, Ham Hill, a large stone quarry, would be swallowed up in a devastating earthquake and that the town of Yeovil would be immersed in a terrible flood. Many local people packed up their families and left the area to stay elsewhere, whilst others packed away their best crockery and clocks in preparation of this natural disaster. On the morning of Good Friday, many people came to gather at Ham Hill to witness Mother Shipton's prediction, but as the 12th hour passed, Ham Hill remained as sturdy as it ever did. The red-faced locals muttered their grievances towards the prophet and returned to their lives.

In Huntspill near Bridgwater, the superstition of the spirit world was documented by writer, James Jennings. In 1810, he wrote about ghostly apparitions returning to their home. In his community, it was believed that if a deceased person was to 'come again' to haunt his home, the only way to lay the spirit to rest was for some cunning men to conjure it away from the house and towards the River Parrett, where the spirit would remain for seven years before returning. He wrote that to remove the spirit permanently was very difficult as it would need to be conjured all the way to the Red Sea.

In Exmoor, Midsummer's Eve on the 23rd June was the evening when many locals would gather in the church in the hope of witnessing the rising of the dead. Local Superstition predicted that spirits of the deceased would rise from their graves and enter the church before returning to their resting place. One father was said to have gone insane after claiming he saw the ghost of his dead daughter rise but not return. In Creech St Michael, locals believed that on Midsummer's Eve, they could see the spirits of those in the parish that would die in the upcoming year. Many would attend the churchyard after fasting and watch to see the spirits pass in the order of which they would perish, each knocking at the church door before vanishing.

Holy water played a part in the superstitions of communities such as Shepton Mallet, where local farmers asked for their cattle to be exorcised and blessed with holy water to send away the devil. Within the family ritual of attending church, many believed that if the clock struck whilst a hymn was being sung, then a parishioner in the congregation would die within a week. This superstition was so strong that many vicars removed the striking mechanism from the church clock before his service began.

Even leaving the church after service had its own risks with many believing that if a congregation left at the same time as a local chapel, then rain would surely follow.

Superstition was prominent in life events such as baptisms, marriage, and death. Not necessarily a local superstition but one held firmly in Somerset was that a baby who screams at a baptism was ridding itself of the devil. While many believed that an infant that was not baptised before death would forever flutter, never finding their way to heaven. A bridesmaid who stumbles while following the bride down the aisle will never marry. If there is an unused open grave at the church on the day of a wedding, this marriage was doomed to fail. The fourth finger of the left hand was believed to have an artery that ran straight to the heart which ensured enduring love, so even considering placing a wedding ring on any other finger was unthinkable.

Superstition in the location of the deceased's burial was rife in Somerset, however, I am unsure whether it was a nationwide superstition. You would not want your loved one buried on the north side of a church. The north side was the common spot for plague victims or criminals. Some believed the sun shone better to the south and the north was shadowed and cold, so they wanted their loved ones in the sunlight. In the village of Stogumber there was a triangular area which is never used for burial and is believed to hold the many bodies of plague victims.

Finding love was the yearning of every Somerset girls' heart and there were many superstitions to aid her in finding a true love and getting him down the aisle. Roses, which are commonly associated with affairs of the heart, were a key object in predicting true love and a woman's future. A girl would close her eyes and select a rose from a mixed bunch of red and white. If she chose a red rose, she would marry a rich man, whilst a white flower meant she would be scrubbing floors and peeling vegetables all her life. If a woman wanted to check her love was true to her, she must fill a cup with running water while saying:

'Water, water running free,

May my love run swift to me.'

She would then gather red and white roses and place them in a heart shape on a table near an open window before bed. In the morning, she should check the flowers and if the roses were still fresh, then her love was true, but if they had faded, then he had another love. To summon a future love, a woman would follow the ritual of walking upstairs backwards whilst carrying a hard-boiled egg and a glass of water. She should place the egg and the water on a chair, and while getting into bed backwards, she should state:

'It's not this egg I mean to eat,

But my true love's heart I mean to seek,

In his apparel and array,

As he wears it every day.'

She must then pretend to sleep, and her true love will appear to drink the water and eat the egg. If a woman were yet to find her future husband, she could place the letters of the alphabet on separate pieces of paper under her bed, upside down in a bowl. The initials of her future love will hopefully float upwards in the morning. Alternatively, she could place a wedding cake under her pillow to induce an image of her future husband in her dreams. If a single woman were to find nine peas in a pod when shelling peas, she should hang the pod and the peas over the door. The first man to enter would be her future husband. Many people in Somerset's rural communities believed that a double yolk in an egg foretold a rushed marriage and an unexpected pregnancy would occur in the household.

There were many dates in the calendar which held superstitions for the people of Somerset. New Year's Day remains the start of a new year and new hopes for the year ahead. We are all aware of the very well-known saying of any laundry washed on this day would wash your luck away, but in West Somerset, the more popular belief was that you must not sweep your dust out the door on this day as you will sweep a loved one away. For a year of good luck, a person should leave the house empty-handed and return with it full, whilst the first man that crossed your threshold on New Year's Day should have a full head of dark hair to bring luck, a sandy or ginger-haired man would bring the opposite. A new baby born into the family on this day would bring luck for the whole family. Whereas the sight of a robin on this day foretold that a member of the household would perish in the coming year.

One Somerset New Year's Day superstition that is mostly obsolete now was using the chapters of the bible to predict what sort of year was ahead. On the morning of New Year's Day, the family bible would be placed on the kitchen table and a person would open it at any random page and place their finger on a chapter. This chapter would then be read out to the family and meaning would be found in the words to predict what joys and trials the family may face that year.

Easter, another popular family celebration, had its own superstitions. Throwing any laundry suds away on Good Friday would bring bad luck as this was throwing suds into the saviour's face, whilst baking bread and sowing seeds would have a successful outcome on this day. On Easter Sunday, many young men would climb the highest hills on the Quantocks or Exmoor to watch the sun rise, this would set him up for a year of good luck. In the Mendip area, it was considered lucky to see a lamb on Easter Sunday morning, whereas at the Blackdown Hills, locals believed if you watched the sunrise on Easter Sunday you would see a lion in the sun. If a man had treated himself to a new hat, then wearing it for the first time on Easter Sunday would protect him from a crow messing on his head.

Christmas also carried superstitions in Somerset. If a West Country maid lays on a bed covered with holly spray on Christmas Eve, she would be visited and punished by evil spirits and goblins. Many believed that having a mince pie at a different house each evening of the 12 advent days would bring 12 lucky months, although some communities substituted the mince pie with Christmas pudding.

Many Somerset superstitions involve animals. The poor hare seems to be constantly linked with bad luck. The hare along with other small wild animals have, for a long time, been associated with witchcraft and the shapeshifting from her true form to that of an animal, but indeed the superstition of the hare goes much further. Many believe that if you cross the path of a hare while embarking on a journey, you should return home as bad luck will surely come your way. A fisherman embarking on a day's work would not go to sea if he saw a hare on his way to work. Likewise, superstition dictates that if a hare is seen in a town or village street, then a building in that town will be ablaze. The hare has also been associated with settling ailments. The blood of a hare was said to remove freckles whilst carrying a hare's front right foot in your pocket could relieve rheumatism.

Many in the county attributed the hare to the treatment of ailments in babies. For fretful babies, feeding it some boiled hare brains would settle it, while babies who were born with deformities  of the mouth were recommended small quantities of hare brain in its mouth. In Chard, it was a well-known superstition that if your baby's soft spot did not close as it should, then the application of a hare's brain could bring this on.

Hares were not the only animal that Somerset communities would use to relieve a child's illness. In some areas, people believed that to cure a baby of thrush in its mouth, you should place a live frog on the infant's tongue. Whooping cough was cured by placing the child into the sheepfold to breathe in the sheep's breath, preferably early in the morning. To strengthen a weak back, rub snails onto the legs. Snails should also be swallowed whole to treat tonsilitis.

Animals were also believed to have the ability to predict death. Both the howling of a dog or the knocking on the window of a bird warned a household that death was coming to its doorstep. In some rural villages, people believed that the crow of a hen predicted a death in the family unless immediately killed and cooked. In West Somerset, hanging a live snake at the front door would ward off epileptic fits, while eels poured down the throat of sick cows would instantly recover an ailing herd. Spiders were perfect for the treatment of fever and shivering and could either be killed, placed in bread and consumed, or alternatively, a live spider placed in a glass of water, once drowned, the liquid should be drank… spider and all!

The cuckoo has a prominent role in Somerset superstition. As the sound of the cuckoo is held as a sign of the arrival of spring, there were many who believed that when the sound of the cuckoo is heard for the first time that year, a person must run up and down the road as fast as they can, and for as long as they can, otherwise they would be lazy for the rest of the year. Other superstitions stated that if you had no money in your pocket when the cuckoo was first heard, you would remain penniless for the rest of the year. If the cuckoo arrived later in April than expected, farmers could expect a year that would be bad for cattle but good for corn. There are also romantic superstitions connected to the sounds of the cuckoo. At the first sound of the cuckoo, a young girl should immediately kiss her hand and ask, 'Cuckoo, cuckoo, when shall I be married?' the amount of calls replied will tell her how many years she must wait for her true love. It was, however, not a good omen to hear a cuckoo whilst in slumber. The saying goes:

'It is well to be dead, then hear the cuckoo in bed.'

Plants too are at the heart of a few Somerset superstitions. In Athelney, a child born with an ailment would be advised to charm away the illness with the aid of a sapling ash. As the sun rose on a summer's morning, the child would be taken to the ash and the sapling would be split down the middle and wedged open. The naked child would then be passed through the sapling's gap with its face toward the heavens. The child would then be dressed, and the sapling bound together. As the sapling grew in the years to come, the child would grow out of his ailment. The Myrtle plant was believed to be the luckiest plant to have in the house. The Myrtus Communis is a fragrant evergreen with small white flowers and was popular in wedding bouquets in the Victorian era. For good luck, the Myrtle would need to be planted by a woman, placed in the window, and always watered in the morning. For the plant to be lucky, it could never be managed by a male and it was said that for her to benefit from the good luck, she would need to 'spread her skirt and look proud!'

Blackberries are a favourite autumnal plant which many of us picked on lazy Sunday afternoons and took back to mum to bake in a crumble. Somerset superstition stated that if you were to trip over the brambles while foraging, this was a punishment from the pixies for stealing their fruit. Whilst others believed that any blackberries remaining after

Michaelmas (29th September) would be destroyed as the devil put his foot on them. Stains on linen caused by fruit were believed to fade as the fruit went out of season. Many believed that a case of the piles could be treated by carrying a conker in the pocket.

The weather too had many superstitions attached to it. Each month of the year seemed to bring its own predictions, and most were centred on farming. If January was warm, then May would be cold. If it thundered in February, the summer would be hot. If it was a fine day on the 26th March, the first day of spring, we would have a beautiful summer, but if it was overcast and wet, then the coming summer would be a washout. In April, the saying goes, 'When April blows his horn, it's good for both hay and corn.' A cold May is kindly and fills the barn finely. Whereas a dripping June brings all things in tune. If on the 1st of July it be rainy weather, it will rain more or less for three weeks together. A dry August and warm does harvest no harm, but fog in August indicates a severe upcoming winter with heavy snowfall. September blow soft till the fruits in the loft. Whilst ice in October will bear up a duck, foretells a winter as wet as muck, whilst thunder in November signifies the next year to be fruitful and merry with cheapness of corn. A December frost and January flood never boded the husbandman's good.

Rain seems to be prominent in the minds of the superstitious in Somerset. For many, I suppose rain is the worst kind of weather and so most superstitions are linked with bad luck. The most bizarre rain-related superstition I have come across is if a German band played in Somerset, they would always bring rain. I have found no explanation for this superstition and it seems to be nowhere else other than in Somerset. More common superstitions include cleaning your windows or killing a spider will bring rain, a black beetle on its back, the sighting of a jackdaw or a braying donkey signifies rain is on the way, however, if a dog is chasing its own tail, then the opposite of whatever weather you are experiencing is on its way. A popular superstition by the Somerset sailor is that if a new moon appears on a Sunday, then a month of rain will follow. Sailors would be just as displeased if a new moon appeared on a Saturday with the saying, 'New moon, sailor's doom'. If a person witnessed rain and sunshine together, then this meant that somewhere in the county witches were making butter.

I will finish this chapter with some superstitions that are a little more random but are as interesting and entertaining as the more common ones.

In South Somerset, it was a common superstition never to walk past a piece of coal that had been dropped on the road. The person should pick the coal up and throw it over his left shoulder to bring good luck. In other parts of Somerset, a piece of coal found on the floor should be carried in your trouser pocket as a charm, and if some lucky person were to find a lump of coal under some mugwort on Midsummer's Eve, then they would be protected from the plague, lightning and burning.

In a West Somerset village (unnamed), if a farmer killed his pig to eat, then said pig could not be salted by his wife if she is with child, because a pig will not take salt from a pregnant woman.

On the highest mound of the hill overlooking Weston-Super-Mare, there was a heap of stones. This area was known as Peak Winnard. Local Fishermen who took the walk from Kewstoke to the sea would contribute one stone to the pile as they passed by to ensure a good day of fishing. As they threw the stone, they muttered:

'Peak Weena, send me a deesh of feesh for me deener.'

In Langport, when the master of the house had died, someone must 'tap the bees'. The bees must be informed that the master had died, otherwise, they would leave and swarm elsewhere.

Also, in Langport, if you drink water from a brook, you must rub the water onto your elbows before taking a sip.

In the village of Over Stowey, the locals suffering from stomach cramps would place a bowl of water under the bed to relieve the ailment.

In North Somerset, if a person discovered a horseshoe discarded in a field, he must throw it over his left shoulder to bring good fortune.

In an unnamed location in Somerset, there was the belief that if two people wash in the same water, they must both spit in it, otherwise, they will soon quarrel. This is similar to the wider known superstition that two women should never pour tea from the same pot, otherwise, one of them would be with child in the next year. It was considered bad manners for a visiting woman to pour tea from her hostess's pot. Any rude visitor that did this would be predicted to be in trouble before the year was out.

When the nose twitches, you will either be kissed, vexed, cursed, or shall shake hands with a fool.

Tingling or hot ears were a sign that someone was speaking your name. The left ear signified bad things were being said, while the right ear indicated your name was used favourably. If the left-eared tingler bit his finger the person speaking slander would bite their tongue.

Removing a loose piece of cotton from another's clothes signifies a letter will be arriving.

To protect yourself from all ails, carry half an onion in your pocket, if the plague is near, then hanging a peeled onion at your front door will protect your family.

Mysterious Unsolved

Murders

Crime in the 19th century is of real interest to me, and I think it is remarkable how the law enforcement at the time, having none of the forensic advances of modern times, investigated crimes and brought many to justice. It is fair to say that many more were likely to have been falsely accused and hanged for crimes they did not commit. This chapter tells the stories of murders that were either left unsolved, or where an open verdict was announced at inquest because of lack of evidence. In some of these stories, I use the word 'unsolved' loosely because, for me as the researcher, it's clear if these stories were tried in modern times with the benefits of forensics, surveillance cameras, and a more uniform style of policing, the people acquitted for these crimes would have, without doubt, faced the hangman. It is important to remember when reading how the inquest juries dealt with the cases and came to their decisions, and in a case of capital punishment, these decisions could literally claim the life of another human. Many would be reluctant to place the crime of murder on someone if they had any doubts. The well-known saying of 'Beyond a Reasonable Doubt' meant a great deal to these juries. It is also important to bear in mind the judges and coroners' attitudes in these times. Historically, the judges' biased summing up would mostly go unchallenged and would influence the jury's decision much more than the facts in some cases.

The Drummer

In December 1809, young man Patrick Chastey was visiting the town of Taunton as a drummer for the 19th foot regiment. Patrick was 22 years old and was lodging at the Three Tuns public house in Tancred street, where the niece of the landlord described him as an incredibly quiet young man. On the evening of 2nd December, Patrick vanished after spending the evening drinking in various public houses with three local men. One month later, his body was found in the river near Creech Mill in Creech St Michael.

Local man Charles Broom discovered the body of Patrick on a cold morning in January 1810. He immediately took the badly decomposed soldier to the New Inn, where surgeon Hugh Standard was immediately summoned. Although the soldier's body was decomposed, it was clear that he wore the visiting regiment's uniform. Corporal James Hogg confirmed his identity, his green uniform still intact but with trousers and shoes badly torn and damaged. The surgeon performed a post-mortem, and even though the soldier had a mark on his forehead clearly inflicted by a violent blow, the surgeon was unable to say with certainty it was the blow to the head and not the possible drowning that caused the young man's death.

With witnesses giving statements of seeing the drummer drinking with local men, Charles Way, an infamous drinker, was taken into custody and an inquest held. However, due to the lack of evidence and the surgeon being unable to distinguish the cause of death, Way was set free, and the verdict of 'found Drowned' was given by the jury.

Twenty-four years later, on the 17th January 1833, local veterinary surgeon Charles Ricketts was enjoying a pint of ale in the George Inn, when an inebriated man named Anthony Gerrard started a quarrel about an elephant. Ricketts had never met Gerrard before but knew he was the landlord of the Black Boy Inn, and rumours around town had said he knew what happened to the drummer boy all those years ago. Taking advantage of his drunken state, Ricketts asked Gerrard what he knew about the Drummer boy. The landlady, Mrs Day, replied it was not Anthony Gerrard that had murdered him but that he knew very well who did it.

Another drinker then shouted across the bar to Gerrard, 'Tell us what had become of the drummer's money.' Gerrard replied that he had neither taken his money nor murdered him but knew he was indeed murdered. He then drunkenly began telling a tale of three local men who had been drinking with the soldier the night he vanished, John Brooks – now a pauper, John Monkton, a local butcher, and Charles Way who had died a few years before. He told the vet the men had enjoyed a game of cards with Patrick and lost a fair bit of money to him. He said he saw the men go off together, and the drummer never returned and he knew he had been killed. Outraged by this tale of murder, Ricketts left the public house to search for a constable. Unable to find one, he returned to the Inn, where Gerrard was waiting for him at the door. Weeping bitterly, Gerrard begged him not to tell anyone what he had said; he vowed to do anything that the man asked in return for his silence. Ricketts pushed him away, telling him to keep his drunken villainous hands to himself.

The next morning, Charles Ricketts reported the man to a local policeman, and a magistrate ordered a warrant for the arrest of John Brooks, John Monkton, and Anthony Gerrard. The three men were kept at Wilton prison, where they underwent three days of interviews by local police. A day later, John Brooks and John Monkton were charged with wilful murder and committed to trial at the spring Assizes. Anthony Gerrard was initially charged as an accessory but later discharged on the order to give evidence at the trial.

On the 6th April 1833, the Western Circuit arrived in Somerset, and the two men accused of murder stood before Justice Parke. Both men claimed their innocence. Many witnesses were provided by the prosecution. Charles Gray, a sieve maker of the town, stated he knew Patrick Chastey from the Three Tuns. He told the court he saw Patrick with the three men on the night he vanished, drinking in both the Squirrel and Shakespeare public houses on East Reach; he noticed Patrick was quite tipsy, and he advised him to go home. He never saw him again. He confirmed that he had heard Gerrard say many times that he did not murder the man but knew who had. Susan Buttell, the niece to the landlord of the Three tuns, told the court Chastey had returned to his lodgings around 11 pm and seemed tipsy; he told her he had been playing cards at the Dolphin. Brooks and Monkton then knocked on the door and called Patrick out into the street. Other witnesses came to the stand to confirm the men were quarrelling out in the street between 11 pm and 12 am the night he vanished.

Simon Mitchell, a local man who lived near the river, then took the stand to say voices had woken him up just after midnight on the day the soldier vanished. Looking through the window, he saw three men talking on the bridge. Curious, he went outside and heard one man say 'he's gone' before walking away, the other two men followed, Monkton carrying a bag; he watched them head towards Cannon Street before returning to his bed. A month later, he heard a body had been found in the river. The surgeon who had carried out the post-mortem in 1809 next took the stand; he explained to the jury there was a mark on the deceased's head which appeared to have come from a violent blow which he felt was inflicted before his death, however, the body was so badly decomposed when found he could not detect any other injuries and could not state if Patrick died of the head wound or of drowning.

Mary Bowyer, the New Inn landlord in 1809, told the court that Patrick's body was brought to her premises by Charles Broom, and the surgeon summoned. At this time, both John Brooks and the deceased Charles Way were present at the public house. She overheard an unnamed man say to Brooks, 'I tell you what it is Brooks, you must know something about the murder of the drummer, for I came out of the Shakespeare and saw you and the drummer together and you were both at angry and hard words. I saw you go over the old plot and you were the last man with him, you know he was murdered!' Brooks did not reply. Police constable Samuel Hackett, then told the jury that when he arrested Charles Day on suspicion of murder in 1809, he had held him at the Squirrel Inn. During the day, John Brooks had attended the public house several times trying to talk to Way, the constable eventually threatened to arrest him for being troublesome if he did not stay away.

Numerous witnesses spoke to the jury of the many times they had overheard Gerrard state he knew who the murderers were. One testified he had heard he and his wife argue in the Black Boy public house, in which she threatened to reveal his secret saying, 'Hang thee, you who murdered the drummer'.

Despite the many witnesses offering evidence of seeing the men together and Gerrard's many years of drunken confession, the judge told the jury that there was no evidence to suggest Patrick Chastey was dealt the blow on his head by another person or if he may have injured himself whilst 'tipsy'. He pointed out that there was no evidence to suggest the man was pushed into the river by another, other than the drunken ramblings of a man who always had a lot to say. He told the jury that if they could not be sure, beyond a reasonable doubt, that these two men caused the death of the drummer by striking him or drowning, then they were compelled to acquit. The jury returned a verdict of Not Guilty.

No one will ever know whether the three men actually caused the death of Patrick or whether he had drunkenly fallen, struck his head and drowned. The men had been drinking all day. There is no question they quarrelled, many witnessed this, but did they strike him? Gerrard stating he saw them leave the area together did not prove they were responsible for Patrick's demise. Did three men get away with murder or did a young man have more ale than he could stand?

A local person told a newspaper at the time that the death of the drummer had tormented Charles Way all the way to his early grave. Guilt? He took the secret with him to his resting place.

Making a murder of it

John Hooper was a 21-year-old lad living in Weston Super Mare and working as a journeyman butcher. His family lived in Bridgwater, but he had family in the Weston area and was engaged to marry his second Cousin Elizabeth Webber, a local servant living in Kewstoke with her father. John was a healthy and well-liked member of the community, so when his body was discovered on a cold frosty January morning in 1865 on a hill in Worlebury woods, it shook the community and became national news.

William Dyer was a local forester at Ashcombe Farm and had lived in this area for many years. He had seen many things in his years of work, but this was the first time he had ever discovered a dead body. He found the deceased man just seventy yards from the main road and three yards from the byroad to Kewstoke. He approached the corpse, which lay four foot away from a tree. The deceased was laid on his back, on the cold ground, but in a crooked position, his trousers were undone but his penis not exposed. The man's hat had been placed on his forehead, obscuring his face. Dyer immediately sent for a sergeant. Officers attended the scene and removed the body of the young man, taking him to a public house in Weston.

Once identified, Sergeant Hardwick carefully scrutinised John's movements on the night of his death; there was no evidence of a robbery and no visible signs of a scuffle. The Sergeant discovered that the last person to see John alive was his fiancée Elizabeth. She stated that the two of them had been sweethearts for a while and were engaged to be married. On that Sunday evening, John had walked with her to see her father in Kewstoke, before walking back to Weston Super Mare, in the company of her sister and another young man. Once back at the town, Elizabeth said John had felt unwell and said he would return to his lodgings at market house lane. This was the last time she saw him alive. Elizabeth stated she had no idea why John would have returned to Worlebury hill.

The mystery surrounding the young man's death caused great excitement in the town of Weston, with many speculating he had died at the hands of foul play with a wound to the back of his head. For this community, it seemed impossible for such a healthy young man, who never indulged in any intoxications, but led a steady life training to become a master butcher in a local shop, to have expired due to sudden ill health.

The inquest into Johns death was delayed due to the coroner being unwell but took place at the end of January in the Market House Inn in Weston. The coroner's deputy Mr Biggs filling his shoes in his absence. The inquest had caused a lot of local interest, and the proceedings were very crowded. Mr Biggs began the inquest by stating that although this case had caused a local sensation, he felt there was not much in the matter, with no marks of violence, no evidence of a scuffle and no clear motive of malice by anyone towards the young man. He acknowledged that while it was a sudden death, there was no evidence to indicate foul play or suicide. The jury was taken to view the body, but although Sergeant Hardwick recommended they also visit the location his body was found, the deputy coroner insisted this was not necessary.

First to give evidence was William Dyer, who told the jury how he had discovered the body on that morning. He told them how the man's head was covered with some branches of underwood, and he could see blood coming from both his ears which had settled on the ground around his head. The deceased's right ear appeared swollen. He also stated that he could see footprints of heavy boots leading from the body to the byroad for Kewstoke. These footprints did not match the lightweight boots the deceased was wearing. He said there were no stumps or rocks to have caused a fall and the body was too far from the tree to suggest the man had collided with it in the dark. Mr Dyer suggested to the court that the body had been placed there, as when found, the body was laid in a position which suggested it had been carried over a shoulder and placed down. He also pointed out there was a heavy white frost on the ground, which was apparent under his body too, suggesting that if John Hooper had laid there whilst alive is body heat would have melted the frost.

A local man then came to the stand to state that an independent gentleman who lived at the Royal Terrace had noticed a suspicious man loitering in the woods earlier on the evening John died. He was so alarmed by this mystery man that he turned back from his walk and returned home telling his family about this strange man he had seen.

Charles Hooper, the deceased's father, then took the stand. Charles was a widowed wheelwright from Bridgwater, he spoke to confirm his sons' identity and age and added that he was a strong, healthy man prior to his death. The grief-stricken father told the inquest that he had not seen his son since midsummer (July the year before) but that he had been told his son had been in some trouble regarding the alleged theft of some hay and that an unnamed man had threatened to 'do for him'. Charles confirmed Mr Dyer's evidence that blood had appeared to have flowed from his son's ears at his death. He added he had seen marks on the deceased's chest and neck, which he likened to bruises.

Mr Wookey, the local surgeon that carried out the post-mortem, next gave evidence. He had examined the body at the Market House Inn and said the face of the deceased looked tranquil. His lips had been a purple hue and that there was lividity of the neck (discolouration) which spread to the upper part of the trunk, but there were no signs of violence to explain this. On his head, he could see no injury other than a scratch behind his right ear, from which blood had flowed. He disagreed with other evidence of any blood having flowed from Mr Hooper's ears. He also denied any swelling in the head area and said there was no evidence on the deceased's clothing to suggest there was a struggle although they were very muddy. He went on to describe the post-mortem investigation in which he could find no evidence of a blow to the head, and there was no indication of suffocation although his lungs were congested. All other organs were healthy and the deceased's stomach contents comprised of partially digested food and a small quantity of cider. There was no evidence of any poisoning. He stated that the cause of death in his opinion was that John Hooper died in a comatose state from the exposure to intense cold, and that it is most likely that he was feeling unwell, so he lay down in the woods and had fallen asleep. The deceased's father Charles Hooper then asked the surgeon if he was suggesting that the blood found near the head was from the scratch, to which the doctor replied he was. Charles then stated that he had visited the site, and there was further blood concealed under some leaves. He stated clearly to the inquest that he believed someone had killed his son. A juror questioned Mr Wookey regarding the quantity of blood to which he replied that blood could look much larger in volume than it actually is.

Elizabeth Webber next took the stand, she confirmed she knew the deceased man and that he had been paying his address to her for some time. On that Sunday afternoon she had called at his lodgings and the couple, along with her masters two children, walked to Kewstoke to visit her father. They stayed a while and then returned to Weston. She parted company with John and returned to her workplace and then called for him again at 7 pm. John then accompanied her back to her father's house to visit once more. Later in the evening, John and Elizabeth returned to town again, this time accompanied by her sister and a young man named George Pitman. Elizabeth said that John's manner was odd on the evening walk, he did not speak a single word along the way, and when she asked him if something was wrong, he replied, 'I am poorly Liz'. He did not speak again until they were within 100 yards of his lodgings, to which he said he was returning home because he felt unwell and bid them goodnight. When asked in court, she stated she had no idea what was wrong with him and did not know why his body was discovered a mile and a half in the direction they had just walked from.

Elizabeth told the inquest they had been engaged for two years, were a happy couple and never quarrelled. She said on the Friday before his death he had been very worried due to a misunderstanding over some hay. John had been sent by his master, a butcher in the high street, to Mr Petheram's at Milton to collect some hay for his bullock; he was instructed that if he could not get some there then to go to his master's brother's farm and collect some hay there. Finding no hay at the first location, he followed the instructions given, but a local labourer named John Collard witnessed this and assumed he was stealing it. Collard went straight to Weston and reported this 'theft' to his master. It seemed a misunderstanding between the two brothers led William Lawrence, the butcher's brother to threaten to fetch a constable and have John taken into custody for larceny. John had retold this story to Elizabeth tearfully, saying he would be broken-hearted if he had to appear before a magistrate as he had never been in trouble with the police. The young woman was then quizzed regarding her previous romantic liaisons. She informed the inquest she had had two previous love interests before John, but there was never a cross word between them and John in the couple's two-year engagement. She also confirmed that during their relationship, John had always been a perfect gentleman and never attempted to take liberties with her.

Sergeant Hardwicke informed the inquest that despite lengthy enquiries, no one had made any sighting of John from the time Elizabeth claimed he left her side until the discovery of his body the following morning. At this point, a member of the jury interjected that he did not believe John had left the hill that night and that he had died on that walk back to town, insinuating the involvement of his fiancée. At this accusation, Elizabeth sobbed bitterly saying she solemnly swore she had told the truth as she knew it.

In his summing up, Deputy coroner Mr Biggs stated that although there was a great mystery as to why John had returned to Worlebury woods that night, this did not throw suspicion on any other persons. He was happy with Mr Wookey's explanation of why the death occurred and said that any jury man who was not happy with these findings was in quite a dilemma because they would be obliged to find an alternative explanation for the cause of death. Mr Wookey's official explanation of death was that John Hooper had laid down on the floor because he felt unwell, he had fallen asleep due to this illness and died from the extreme cold – congestion of the lungs being undoubtedly the cause of death. He stated he found no suspicion in Miss Webber's account of John's movements that night and that they must decide based on what evidence they had available to them. The jury retired for forty-five minutes before returning with an open verdict – found dead. They stated the lack of evidence did not satisfy any other conclusion.

The findings of this inquest failed to satisfy John's father Charles and many local townspeople. Speculation continued to circulate as to how he met his tragic end, and local newspapers printed that additional police were being called in to investigate, they also printed that Elizabeth Webber had been arrested, which was found to be untrue. On the 4th February, The Bristol Mercury printed a letter written by Charles Hooper in which he stated that his son's death had not been investigated thoroughly. He demanded that the inquest finding be discounted and a new review begun. In his letter, he asked why George Pitman and Elizabeth's sister had not been questioned by the police and did not appear at the inquest. He questioned James Wookey's findings, stating that there were other witnesses who could confirm blood had flowed from inside both ears and that Johns necktie and scarf were stiff with dried blood. He had visited the scene and claimed to have found blood two inches from the body, the quantity not consistent with that which would flow from a scratch. He also stated that he had seen marks of a thumb and fingers on his deceased son's neck and collar area. He went on to claim Johns right ear was swollen and he had unexplained scratches on his chin. Charles Hooper concluded his letter stating that he believed someone was withholding information about his sons last hours and that he had not died of natural causes. Charles's letter caused quite a stir. It was not the done thing to call into question the opinion and testimony of a surgeon or coroner. National newspapers began printing the story and the higher classes of Weston began taking an interest, concerned about public safety and the reputation of their prospering seaside town.

On the 6th February, the Western Daily Press printed a statement given by Mr Wookey, who not only worked for the coroner and the local hospital but also relied on private custom. In his statement, he said he had been the victim of malicious and vindictive attacks by anonymous correspondents. He wrote that his expertise was of more value than the speculation of newspapers and this personal attack was unacceptable. He informed that three other medical men from the town had now viewed the deceased's body and all agreed no violence played a part in John Hooper's death. Mr Wookey ended his statement by pointing out that at the inquest, he had preserved himself from suggesting that the last act of the deceased's life was an act of immorality (referring to the unbuttoned trousers) out of respect for the family.

Any efforts by Mr Wookey to settle this matter were sadly fruitless, and suspicion and mistrust grew amongst the local people towards both the coroner and the doctor. Just three days after the doctor's statement, a petition was filed by Charles Hooper, and it was greatly supported by the poorer inhabitants of Weston Super Mare. The petition repeated Charles concerns regarding the stark difference in witness statements to Mr Wookey's findings, the footprints and blood at the scene of the death, and how his son could have placed his hat so carefully upon his forehead if in a state of illness. The petition concluded –

'In the interest of truth, justice and humanity, sympathy for the friends of the deceased as well for the safety of the inhabitants of the town, we respectfully urge that a detective be employed to investigate the matter further, a reward be offered, and the home secretary informed'.

As Charles's demand for a more thorough case steamed ahead, the Reverend William Carus- Wilson threw his support behind the demand for the magistrate to intervene, and Charles Hooper began to receive legal threats from Mr Wookey. A trust was initiated in an effort to ask the towns people to donate to Mr Hooper's fight for justice. Any hope by the officials that this saga may fizzle itself out was thwarted when the trust began to receive donations, mostly from the lower class members of the town. At the beginning of March 1865, an internal enquiry began at the Royal Hotel, this was a closed meeting and was attended by forty of the area's gentlemen of influence. This covert enquiry rolled on through the month and was fuelled by a statement made by Sergeant Ballentine in which he stated that in reviewing the evidence and the deceased's body, he believed John Hooper met his death by violence of some kind.

The town continued to be enthralled by this suspicious demise of a young man, but also became the ridicule of many newspapers who claimed this was an attempt to make the town more notorious and well known. The publications became so derogatory that on the 21st April there was a public meeting held at the town hall. Many people attended to hear the chairman of the trust, Mr Jones, defend this seaside town against tabloid scrutiny. He addressed an article that had appeared in the Bristol Times which had stated-

'Our friends at Weston are resolved not to be disappointed of a murder up on the hill. They will only have it that the young man Hooper was foully done to death and having public meetings today to make a murder of it. Well if anyone has been murdered, we hope they find the perpetrator of the crime, but seeing that there are unfortunately too many real murders to be deplored, we think it is a pity they should take so much

trouble to make out one which (we think despite Sergeant Ballentine's opinion) has certainly more the character of natural or accidental death.'

Mr Jones responded that he resented any suggestion that the town revelled in the thought of a murder in their community. He reassured the town that he wanted nothing more than for this case to be found to be a death of natural causes, however this case had many questions unanswered and the town could not rest until these were resolved and answers given to John Hooper's family. The Reverend Carus-Wilson then told the gathering that they had raised £57 6s 7d for the fund (around £3,900 in today's equivalent) and this money had come entirely from the pence of the poor. Considering the solicitor's bill currently sat at £73, he hoped the more fortunate of the town would also contribute. He continued to say that there was now information which he could not share due to legal limitations that he believed if presented to a jury, along with Sergeant Ballentine's opinion, would lead to further investigation and possibly an arrest. He stated he now had written statements from those who witnessed the blood in the ear and marks to the neck and that these men had no reason to state what is untrue. He also stated he had acquired witnesses who confirmed John did not return to Weston with Miss Webber on the night he died and remained on the hill. He urged the locals to be guided by the eminent criminal counsel of Sergeant Ballentine and to ignore the papers negative reports of their town. He concluded that the decision to pursue this request for an enquiry must rest with the inhabitants of the town. The end of this meeting was met with an agreement that a committee of 12 persons be appointed, who shall take charge of all evidence, gather learned counsels opinion and any other related papers. The trust was to continue to canvas the town for funds to pay for the inquiry of the death of John Hooper with a view to satisfying the public's mind.

On the 25th April 1865, Mr Wookey resigned from his duties to the local hospital and any services to the coroner. A few days later, Elizabeth Webber brought Charles Hooper before the magistrate for harassment and slander. In court, she stated Charles had been to her father's house at Kewstoke and entered the house without announcing himself. She told the judge he had taken a locket from her which contained an image of John Hooper and refused to give it back. She said her father had to help her get it back during which time Charles said to Elizabeth 'Why don't you tell the truth?' she replied that she already had, to which he replied ' No you have not, I have proof of it'. He had also said to her father 'how about the murder on the hill, your daughter knows about it.'

Miss Webber said that Charles Hooper was no longer working and spent his days knocking on the doors requesting funds to pay his legal fees. Miss Webber's counsel, Mr Smith, implied that this was the habit of a tramp and perhaps he could be removed back to Bridgwater under the Vagrancy act. Miss Webber went on to say he had also spread rumours that she was walking out with a man named Burgess, which was quite untrue. When quizzed by the defending counsel, she stated that she was not in any bodily fear of Charles Hooper, but his harassment was most unpleasant. Charles Hooper argued he only wanted to take a likeness of the image in the locket as he did not have one. He agreed to stay away from Miss Webber and her family, and the case was dismissed.

The following day, another public meeting was held, in which the chairman instructed that a decision needed to be made on the next course of action. The three choices were to apply for the Queen's bench to quash the original inquest finding, or to take the evidence they had to arrest an unnamed person, or to petition the home secretary for a criminal enquiry. The committee agreed to petition the home secretary. Reverend Carus- Wilson also made a point at this meeting that the deceased's father was in no way a tramp as implied at the court and he had personally provided accommodation for him while he remained in Weston.

On the 16th May, Elizabeth Webber brought Charles Hooper before the magistrate for a second time, accusing him, once again, of harassment. She said he was constantly bothering her, accusing her of hiding information about Johns death. She claimed he shouted in the street to her 'John Hooper was struck down while he was leaning on your arm, if you have any regard for John then tell the truth'. She continued to deny any involvement in her fiancé's death. The judge's refusal to allow Charles Hooper's counsel to cross-examine Miss Webber was met with jeers and grunts of disgust from the spectating crowd. Again, Charles Hooper agreed to keep the peace, and the case was dismissed. As Elizabeth Webber left the court, she was followed through Regent Street and Orchard Place by a large crowd, all shouting accusations of her part in John Hooper's death.

As the town continued to receive ridicule from the national papers, one in which suggested this case would no doubt affect the destination as a place of recreation, the support from the gentlemen of the town began to dwindle. On the 25th May, the committee was suspended as the costs of the case were growing and the donations to the fund greatly reduced. Relying purely on the donations of the poor could only last a short while when they themselves lived on such a limited income. By the beginning of June, the case had completely lost momentum, Reverend Carus-Wilson was away in Devon but wrote a letter in a local paper informing that the petition for the home secretary did not have enough signatures and that it would be better to submit it without then than not to submit at all. Another paper reported that the evidence gathered by the committee was not enough to instruct an arrest of someone who they surmised is accused by a motive of jealously. Then just like that, the story abruptly ended. No further mention of the case in the newspapers and it appears that Charles Hooper returned home to Union Street in Bridgwater.

This story is truly mysterious. The fact that the pursuing of a conclusion was so abruptly abandoned by the committee and local people seems as mysterious as the case itself. So, was John Hooper killed? It is reasonable to see why the coroner and doctor were happy with the conclusion that he was unwell and stopped to rest, It seems plausible a man might place his hat over his face when lying down to sleep and even if unwell he would most likely be able to do this. Elizabeth Webber's version of events would also match with this theory of him complaining of feeling unwell on the way home. The doctor was correct in that congestion of the lungs could be caused by exposure to cold but this did not explain what had caused John to lay down in the first place. Elizabeth Webber did not mention any physical symptoms in John, such as breathlessness or chest pain, and it seems strange that when John told her he felt poorly, she did not pursue this any further with him. Although they walked together for forty minutes, she was unable to tell the inquest in what way he felt poorly. A loved one's expected response would surely be to ask what is ailing them. With regards to the marking on John Hooper's neck and upper chest, it is possible this was discolouration caused by the process of gravitation of blood when the person ceases living, as Mr Wookey and seemingly his three medical men believed. However, this lividity of the skin would not normally look like bruises. It was however only Charles Hooper who mentioned thumbs and finger marks, unlike the blood in the ears, there were no other claims of these marks.

Evidence given by William Dyer, who found the body, pointed towards John Hooper succumbing to foul play. His suggestion that the body was placed there after Johns death is supported by the footprints, the undisturbed frost under the body, and the way in which he claimed that it was laid out. Why were John's trousers undone? Did he stop for a pee and was grabbed from behind? Was the doctor's insinuation that he was in the woods to carry out the immoral act of masturbation true? Was he disturbed? Would a man so fearful of going before the magistrate commit an indecent act in a public place? Seems unlikely.

Charles Hooper's theory clearly was that Elizabeth Webber either initiated or carried out the murder of his son. There were whispers of previous loves and jealously being the motive, certainly, Elizabeth was the last person to see him alive and only she, her sister and a male friend could prove that John ever left the woods. Was the story about the hay stealing a decoy as to why John had been so upset in the days leading to his death? Was the truth that he knew their relationship was coming to an end? Was he making it difficult for her to end the engagement? Was she, as his father stated, walking out with another man? There is no way to answer these questions now. In the modern world, we have CCTV and forensics and a much more sophisticated understanding of the human body. Perhaps if this mystery occurred one hundred years later, Charles Hooper could have gone to his grave with the certainty of how his son met his death.

With regards to the social movement that occurred In Weston Super Mare as a result of Johns death, 1865 was a time when expertise and professionalism went unquestioned, for Charles Hooper to challenge what he did not believe was a true testament to the love of a grieving father. Weston Super Mare was the seaside town of the area and had grown in popularity as social changes brought more recreational time for Victorians. But in the backdrop of that postcard image, there were many poor members of the town who felt overlooked and hidden away. When a working-class father had his concerns overlooked and disregarded by officials, they rose up and demanded that his questions be taken seriously.

It seems most likely that powerful figures in the local area brought an end to the newspaper coverage of the story, and this was likely for two reasons. The newspapers, also shocked that a working-class man contradicted the experts, began painting the people of the town as a melodramatic bunch, rubbing their hands together at the thought of a murder in their town. Secondly, it was so damaging to the reputation of a town that increasingly relied on the tourist trade to boost local business. As a seaside town, Weston Super Mare was still in its infancy as a tourist attraction. The town's hotel, The Royal, only built forty years before this mysterious death. It will never now be known whether John Hooper died of illness or foul play, questions such as why he returned to the woods and did Elizabeth Webber instigate his death will never be answered now. Worlebury Woods would go on to be the scene of several other terrible unsolved murders.

The poisoning of Matilda Hicks

Matilda Hicks was a 77-year-old widow who had lived in the village of Lympsham all her life. She had married later in life to a prosperous local farmer named Ferdinando Hicks and had only one daughter who died aged six. Having sadly lost her only chance at motherhood, Matilda was very close to her brothers' children, particularly her niece Maria who she looked on as an adopted daughter. In 1875, her husband died, leaving her a widow at the age of 68. Fortunately, her late husband's successful farm left her with the means to live comfortably into her elderly years. For a time, she lodged with a local family before moving in the early 1880s into her now married nieces' home. Maria had married a prosperous local farmer and had two sons, Rowland and Hedley, for whom Matilda was very fond of. The family lived at Batch Farm, where they had a successful farming business. The family gave her two rooms on the first floor as a sitting room and bedroom, and in return, she paid £50 per year to Maria's husband John Frost Arney Day.

On the evening of the 6th November 1884, the family's governess, Emily Isabella Stallard, prepared a bowl of oatmeal gruel for the elderly resident. Matilda liked to have a light meal of oatmeal every evening before she settled for bed, especially on the chilly November evenings. The governess made the gruel, delivered a pint of ale to Mr Day, and then went upstairs to prepare the children for bed. Just a few moments later, Matilda came to the landing and said, 'Did you put something in my supper?' to which Miss Stallard replied she had not. Matilda told her there was something in it and asked her to try it. Miss Stallard refused, stating she did not like oatmeal and went to speak to her mistress. Niece Maria came to her aunt and asked what was wrong. Matilda replied, 'I don't know Maria, but something is in that supper and its stinging my throat'. Maria took the bowl away and examined the contents, noticing a red tinge at the bottom of the food. She called for her dressmaker and friend, Martha Sherring, who was visiting the house to measure for a new frock. The two women were then joined by Maria's husband John, who stated the red looked like clotted blood, Martha disagreed, likening it to more of a powder and warned the others not to take it.

In the minutes that followed, Matilda began to feel unwell, experiencing stomach pain, nausea, and a burning throat. Maria instructed her charwoman Mary Sperring (mother of Martha the dressmaker) to nurse the elderly woman in her bedroom whilst her husband John, who frequently suffered from head pain, took a funny turn in the lounge.

Within twenty minutes, Matilda Hicks was dead. Surgeon of Brent Knoll, Dr Alworth Merewether Bayliffe, was sent for immediately and confirmed the elderly woman's death. Dr Bayliffe had known Matilda Hicks for many years, and although advanced in years, he knew her to be in good health. Asking for the dish and its contents, the doctor was horrified to discover that John Day had ordered for it to be cleaned. Going out to the trough, he managed to scrape a small amount of the gruel, which he secured in a bottle. By this time, John Day had taken to his bed, saying he felt unwell with gout. Doctor Bayliffe visited his room before he left the house to ask why he had thrown the questionable oatmeal away. John replied he was fearful one of his children might touch it and suffer the same fate as poor old Matilda. John Day asked the doctor for a certificate of death for the recently deceased, and the doctor replied this would not be possible as the coroner and police would have to be told of this suspicious and unexpected death. John replied that this was nothing but a great bother and nuisance to his family.

An inquest into Matilda's death was immediately launched, and with the help of Doctor George Smith from Axbridge, a post-mortem was carried out. Governess Emily Isabella Stallard told the coroner Mr Craddock and the jury that on that evening she had been preparing Matilda's oatmeal Gruel as she did every evening, using the same pan and implements. She said she poured the gruel into a blue dish and then was asked by her master John Day to fetch him some ale. This only took two minutes, and once she returned with his ale, she added sugar and cream to the gruel and then took the food to the elderly woman. When she arrived at the room, Matilda was sat in darkness, a habit she had developed recently, and so she placed the bowl on the table and went to fetch a candle. Returning with light, she entered the woman's room and placed her dinner in front of her saying 'I brought you your supper', before leaving the room to get the two children ready for bed. She told the court that when delivering the food, she noticed no unusual colouring to the gruel, she also stated that at times Matilda would stir some brandy into the gruel, however she did not witness her doing this on the evening of her death. She confirmed that her master had been in the kitchen several times while she prepared the gruel but that when she went for the ale, she was only gone for two minutes and that when she returned John Day was sat in the same place, seemingly not to have moved.

Mary Sperring, charwoman who was working at the house that evening, testified that she had seen the bowl of food and confirmed some red colouring at the bottom of the bowl and pink powdery colouring around the sides. She confirmed that the deceased had eaten possibly three or four spoons before complaining of burning in her throat. Mr Day had told her to take the bowl and its contents to the pump trough and clean it thoroughly, and he accompanied her carrying the candle whilst she did so. Mrs Day then asked her to tend to Matilda Hicks, she stayed with her and described her to be suffering with severe stomach pain, shaking with discomfort but remaining coherent and in her senses until two minutes before her death.

Doctor Alworth Merewether Bayliffe next appeared before the court and told of his arrival at the house, the conversation he had with John Day, and his discovery that the food thought to have caused the death had been discarded. He told how he collected a sample from the trough and this, along with the deceased's stomach, Liver and kidney had been sent to the county Analyst for testing. With regards to the post-mortem, he confirmed that the deceased was well-nourished and considering her age, had healthy functioning organs.

The case was then adjourned to wait for the return of the analysis of the stomach, and considering all available evidence, the local police felt it was undeniable that Matilda Hicks had met her death by foul means. On the 17th November, John Day and Emily Stallard were brought to Axbridge Court, and under a warrant, charged with wilfully and feloniously and with malice aforethought murdering Matilda Hicks, a 77-year-old widow. Both were remanded into custody to be held at the Axbridge lock- up while the results from the county analyst were eagerly awaited. The county analyst Mr Alford was not happy with the results he had discovered and so sent the remains onto Dr Stephenson of Guy's hospital in London for further investigation. This delay meant that both John Day and Emily Stallard sat in custody for over two weeks.

On the 8th December, the court reconvened at the town hall in Axbridge. Mr Webster appeared for public prosecution, and both John and Emily had their own counsel. Mr Webster told the court that he had been advised there was no evidence against Miss Stallard, and he requested she be immediately discharged and admitted instead as a witness for the prosecution. By the 13th December, the results of the analysis were returned from London and Strychnine was confirmed in Matilda's stomach, liver, and brain. There was also evidence of the poison in the sample the doctor had collected from the family's trough. The inquest could now determine officially that Matilda's death was caused by the administration of a fatal dose of Strychnine. John Frost Arney Day was charged with wilful murder and placed at Shepton Mallet prison to await a criminal trial.

John Day's trial began on the 21st January 1885 at the Taunton Assizes. A large crowd of people gathered at the court, wedging themselves into the gallery, with the entrance blocked and no room for movement. Mr Day was brought to court in a covered vehicle to avoid any contact with the onlookers and when stood in the dock, requested a chair as he felt so unwell. Doctor Bayliffe first appeared for the prosecution, repeating the evidence he had previously given the coroner and adding that a few years ago John Day had suffered a violent kick to the head and had since then complained of chronic head pain. During these bouts of pain, Mr Day suffered from irritability, depression of the spirits, indigestion, and insomnia. Although the doctor considered Mr Day to be a kind man and had witnessed him treating his wife very well, he could also be very irritable and impatient with his family. On the day of Matilda's death, he found Mr Day in bed, complaining of pain, and feeling nauseous, he was very excited in his manner and seemed very eager to acquire a death certificate for his wife's aunt. Mr Day remained in bed for several days after Matilda's death complaining of irritation of the stomach.

Police Constable Thomas Perry gave evidence of the discovery of a blue powder in the kitchen cupboard when he searched the house. The powder was labelled 'poison for mice'. While searching the deceased's bedroom, in the company of Dr Bayliffe, he found a white powder in the bedroom drawer. The constable confirmed that no red powder was discovered in the search of the house.

Martha Sperring, a local dressmaker, and friend of the family confirmed her presence at the house that day. She told the court she had been in the corner of the dimly lit kitchen pressing a dress for Mrs Day while Miss Stallard prepared the gruel. She said she saw John Day come into the kitchen to remove his dirty boots, when Miss Stallard left to get his ale, she witnessed him stirring something into the bowl of gruel, before the governess returned and took the bowl away. When asked why she never mentioned this vital evidence when she had spoken to Doctor Bayliffe, she said she did not realise the relevance of the information at that time. Mr Days defence counsel Mr Clifton cross-examined Martha Sperring very aggressively and at great length regarding this new evidence, but Martha remained insistent at her account and told the court she bore no bad feeling towards Mr Day and was telling the truth. Miss Stallard was asked about Martha's presence in the kitchen and stated she had not seen the dressmaker working in the corner but did agree the room was very dimly lit with only one candle and the fire for light.

Neighbour Martha Cook next took the stand for the prosecution and said she had known Matilda Hicks all her life. The day before she died, she was in perfect health, although she did complain of a headache. Martha said she arrived at the house after Matilda had taken ill and found Mary Sperring cradling her in her last minutes of life. She instructed Mr Day to send for a doctor to which he replied he would in a few minutes, she told him it must be immediate and sent a man herself. When she arrived, she found Mr and Mrs Day in the parlour room. Offering Maria Day help, she was asked to go and help with her aunt because she could not leave her husband as he felt very unwell. After Matilda died, Martha Cook said she removed two purses and a piece of paper from the deceased's pocket. By this time Mr and Mrs Day were in their bedroom, and she testified that as she approached to give the purse to them, she overheard Mrs Day say 'I can't do it John,' but she did not know what this conversation was about.

The prosecutor Mr Clifton summed up the case, stating that he believed John Day murdered his wife's aunt to receive the inheritance. There was evidence that Matilda was planning to leave the Days and stay elsewhere and that John Day was concerned he and his wife may fall out of favour in the deceased's will. He also provided proof that John had borrowed £300 from the deceased a little while ago and was well aware that she owned substantial property. He completed his case by stating that the Day household was such a close-knit one that any disagreement or wrong-doing could be easily concealed.

John Day's defence responded that there was no motive for him to commit this crime against his wife's aunt. She paid him a monthly sum to live at the house, and he knew his wife would benefit from Matilda Hick's death at some point in the future. There was no evidence of financial issues; in fact, the bank had said Mr John Day was a regular and trustworthy customer. He cast serious doubt over the evidence given by Martha Sherring that she had seen him stirring something. Pointing out that Miss Stallard had been a key witness in this trial, and she could not confirm that Miss Sherring was in the kitchen. Even if she had been working in the corner unnoticed, he argued the kitchen was too dimly lit to say with certainty that she saw Mr Day stirring something at the table. The judge stated there was no doubt that Matilda Hicks died from Strychnine poisoning, but there was no evidence of a red powder in the house. He instructed the jury they should only find John Day guilty of Wilful murder if they are certain, beyond a reasonable doubt, that he and no one else had placed the poison in the gruel. If they cannot be certain of this, they should acquit. The Jury deliberated for one hour before returning a verdict of not guilty, and John Day was acquitted. As he left the court, he was mobbed by an angry crowd who were certain this man had just got away with murder.

The Day's placed the land and property of Matilda Hick's estate up for sale on the 7th March and by the end of the year had left England for New Zealand with their two sons. They never returned to the United Kingdom. Matilda Hick's murder was never solved.

It is clear that someone in that house that night had added Strychnine to Martha's gruel. Means, opportunity, and motive are the basis in which all murders are considered, and in this case, this was blurry. Did Miss Stallard have a reason to want Matilda gone? It appeared not. John Day owed Matilda money, but there was no indication of financial troubles. Did Martha the dressmaker witness him stirring something into the bowl? And why did he really discard of the gruel so hastily? Was it really to protect his two sons? It is interesting that niece Maria did not seem to come under any suspicion and was not asked to provide any evidence in court. The solicitor commented that this family were a close-knit one and there could be many things going on behind closed doors that could be hidden from the outside world. Did the household really live alongside each other as peacefully as they claimed? We will never know.

Who murdered Elsie Luke?

On Friday 29th September 1893, two young boys made a grisly discovery whilst playing at Hampton Down in Bath. Whilst exploring the area, they discovered a small cavern that could only be accessed on their knees, crawling in, the children found a skeleton laying there with only a small piece of flesh remaining, the skeleton was wrapped in a linen cloth and covered in large flat stones. The macabre discovery was reported to the local police who quickly attended and removed the body, which was positioned on its right side with arms and legs tucked in. Further investigation showed that the skeleton was of a female in her mid-twenties, the woman had been of a small build, and some remaining flesh on the scalp showed light brown hair. Her skull showed an indentation that indicated she had been struck with violence, and there were fractures to her foot and leg. Fragments of clothing on the body and the linen wrapped around were marked with the word 'Kerry'. The Kerry family of Cheriton house were contacted, and they revealed that a disgraced cook, Elsie Luke, had vanished two years ago.

Elizabeth Luke, alias Wilkie was known as Elsie. She was born in London in 1867. At the age of 13, Elsie was arrested and charged with theft and sent down to the south-west to the Limply Stoke reformatory. She remained there until 1885 and once released decided to stay in the area. Elsie found work in Bath as a cook to private households and remained in touch with the school. It seems that Elsie had two persona's, to the people that employed her she came across as a well-educated girl with a highly nervous disposition and a strong cockney accent, however, those that knew her socially knew her to be a shrewd thief who forged character references to gain respectable positions. In 1891, Elsie was working at Cheriton House, home of the Kerry family, but by July she was served a months' notice to leave as the family suspected her of stealing from the house. Elsie asked Mr Kerry if she could be released earlier as she had a dying relative in London that she needed to tend to, her employer agreed and gave her the remaining wages. But Elsie remained in Bath, staying at various people's houses before vanishing, her acquaintances thought she had returned to her family in London.

How did this young woman meet her gristly death? Why would someone kill a 27-year-old woman and conceal her body in a cave? The police immediately began investigating and discovered that two years before, a watch and chain, cufflinks and a bloody handkerchief were found in a neighbouring cave to Elsie's resting place by a man named Mr Dill. The man did not take these items to the police station but instead sold the watch and chain at the Exeter Inn, and he kept the cufflinks and handkerchiefs. The police were able to retrieve the watch from the buyer and took all items as evidence. The handkerchief was found to bear the initials of Mrs Kerry. Another witness came forward saying he had found a black straw hat with a cream trim on the downs two years before, and he had handed this into the police station, but mistaking this for unclaimed lost property, the hat was destroyed. The same witness told how on the day he found the hat he was picnicking with friends and saw a young man in a shirt and no hat. The man looked hurried and said he had been swimming in the river Avon and someone had stolen his belongings to explain his dishevelled appearance.

After further statements were taken by Elsie's acquaintances, a 20-year-old man named Arthur Stephenson Coombs was arrested. Arthur was a native of the area and lived just a few doors from Elsie's employment with his parents. Arthur was a coachbuilder apprentice, and although only seventeen, was extremely popular with the ladies. At his arrest, he asked how they could be sure the skeleton was Elsie, to which the arresting officer told him the Kerry's had positively identified the linen cloth and undergarment Elsie had stolen from their home. He then responded 'I did not do it. I kept company with her. But after that, I am no use to you'. At the station, he admitted he had been seeing another female servant and Elsie had been very angry about this. She had been spreading rumours she was pregnant with his child.

Arthur Coombs was arrested on suspicion of murder on the 29th September. The inquest into Elsie's death ran alongside the criminal investigation. The inquest began at The George Inn in Bathampton at the end of September. The details of the case were laid out before the coroner. The identifying undergarments found on her body and her subsequent disappearance which matched the date the surgeon suspected the person had died, satisfied all concerned that the skeleton in the cave was definitely Elsie Luke. Many witnesses came forward, offering insight into the difficult relationship that had developed between Elsie and Arthur. The girl's co-worker stated that Elsie would have a male visitor to her workplace regularly, and she always took him down to the cellar. Another witness said they saw Elsie stood outside of Arthurs house two days before the last sighting of her, which was provided by local woman Annie Hayman. She testified that she had seen Elsie walking towards the city at 5 pm on the August bank holiday Monday.

When discussing the condition of the skeleton, Dr Harper the examining surgeon, stated he felt the indentation to the skull, and the fractures to the leg suggested she had been struck with great violence by a small item and then thrown into the quarry. He could not confirm whether the cause of death was caused by the blow to the head or the subsequent fall. A witness named John Edwards, a local fishmonger, then gave evidence saying he had a conversation with Arthur in which he asked why he does not ever see him with that girl, to which he had responded 'She ought to be dead or killed'. Two further witnesses came forward stating they had seen Elsie and Arthur walking together that summer.

Evidence was then given from a police officer who searched Arthur's room at the time of his arrest. Besides a brooch identified as belonging to Elsie, a large package of letters was found in his room from various women, although none from the deceased. Within this package, there were many letters from a woman named Polly Sheppard, whom he had also been seeing when he kept company with Elsie and to whom he was now engaged. In these letters, Polly wrote about her anger at Elsie's allegations of pregnancy, reassuring him his parents would know it was a lie. As her letters went on, she became increasingly hostile towards Elsie, mocking her clothing and behaviours. In a letter dated 5th April 1891, Polly wrote,

'That girl thinks she is going to mar our happiness but she is mistaken. Emma seen her run up and seen her stare black as though she was mad. A lunatic. She cannot do anything else or she would not act so silly. She had not better say anything or she will know the reason why. I shall let her know she is talking to someone better than her.'

The inquiry also heard that on the 7th August Arthur had attended the Bath hospital for treatment for a human bite to his thumb, which he said he had got when he had a fight with an unknown man at a liberal fete. The case was again adjourned, and Arthur Coombs kept in police custody.

In October 1893 Arthur returned to court, by this time the case had grown country wide interest and hundreds of excited people gathered outside the court, pushing, shouting and clamouring to get a spot in the courthouse, the police struggling to maintain control. In the courtroom, the prosecution suggested that this 20-year-old Lothario had become entangled with two headstrong, demanding women and needed to rid himself of one of them. He highlighted witness statements that Polly and Elsie had an intense dislike for each other which on one occasion broke out into a skirmish in which Polly was thrown to the floor. Mary Louisa

Sheppard, known as Polly, then provided evidence stating that although she was aware of Arthurs reputation with women, she loved him dearly and was looking forward to their forthcoming marriage. She also provided an alibi for Arthur, stating they were at the Theatre together on the evening Elsie disappeared. When asked why she had not disclosed this when she was first asked, she said she was not sure.

On the 17th October 1893, a lack of evidence meant that Arthur was released from police custody by the magistrate, the next month he then made an appearance at the inquest in an effort to exonerate himself from any accusations of murder. This was the first time Arthur was given the opportunity to publicly offer his account of the situation. He told the jury that he had kept company with Elsie Luke but had ended the relationship in February 1891 when he discovered she had secured her position in the Kerry household with a fraudulent character reference. He said he only called at Cheriton House to see her on two occasions and never entered the house or went to the cellar. He claimed that he was not involved with Elsie after February and that any persons stating they saw them together in the summer of 1891 were mistaken. He testified that the couple had never been intimate and that he did not see her on the days leading up to her disappearance. He recounted his movements on the August bank holiday in line with Polly's account, adding that he had gone on a long walk during that day with a young woman named Miss Thorne. He confirmed the story he had provided earlier for the injury to his thumb and added that the only reason he had the brooch in his room was that Elsie had asked him to repair it. The inquest was again adjourned for further investigation.

When the case resumed at the Parochial Hall in Bathampton at the end of November, Arthurs mother and brother both took the stand. Mrs Coomb told the inquest that Elsie had visited her home at 25 Kingsmead Terrace in February 1891. In the presence of her husband and two sons, she claimed that Arthur had taken liberties with her in the Royal Victoria Park and that she was now with child, although there was no physical proof of pregnancy. Arthur denied these allegations and Elsie left the house. Mrs Coombs also confirmed Arthurs alibi for his movements on the bank holiday, saying that she witnessed him return from the Theatre at 11 pm. His older brother William Henry then took the stand and confirmed he could remember his brother walking out with the young woman. He had felt this was unwise as Elsie was known to have a dubious character and the brothers had two or three conversations which he advised his brother to end any friendship with her. William confirmed his mother's story that Elsie had come to the house in February; he said she knocked violently at the door and refused to leave until she was granted an audience with her lover's parents. When she made her claims of pregnancy, William had asked her why she would allow a seventeen-year-old boy to take liberties with her, being six years older, to which she responded Arthur had lied about his age. William reported that he told her if her story were true, then she should return when her pregnancy was more obvious, and the family would address the issue. Elsie never returned. A rather odd woman named Elizabeth Lane then offered evidence to a sighting of a couple on the August bank holiday. She told the court she had witnessed a woman in an ill-fitting dress and a black straw hat being led across the grass by a slim man with boyish looks. She stated the reason it stuck in her mind was that the dress she wore was incredibly drab. Whilst giving this evidence, the eccentric woman was very garbled and seemed confused and disorientated which caused some amusement to the proceedings, the judge then stated it would be better to discount her evidence as she was not a reliable witness. The case was again adjourned awaiting further evidence.

The inquest into Elsie Adeline Luke's death reached its conclusion on the 6th December 1893 in a large room at the George Inn at Bathampton. Coroner Samuel Craddock first heard from a gentleman from the Royal Institute regarding the rainfall on the August weekend, and although it had been showery, it was agreed that the suggestion of an accident and slipping on a muddy ground into the quarry could not explain Elsie's death. The last witness was a policeman who was present at the liberal fete in which Arthur alleged he had this thumb bitten in a fight. This officer stated he had witnessed no animosity between anyone that day and witnessed no fights.

The coroner then began summing up this intriguing and frustrating case to prepare the jury in making their decision. He told them that there was no doubt in his mind that Elsie was murdered. There was no possible way she could have placed herself in the cave, and her injuries undoubtedly indicated a violent blow to the head, followed by a fall. He drew attention to the only possible suspect Arthur Stephenson Coombs and a clear motive of needing to remove a woman who was causing great problems to him and his family. He stated it was clear that some form of a relationship had taken place between them and it was up to them to consider Coombs claims that he had no contact with her after February, which was contrary to witnesses accounts of seeing them together that summer. He warned the jury to ignore outside influence in their consideration of Coombs character and that although it was clear he had contact with other woman whilst engaged to Polly Sheppard, this did not mean he was a murderer. His final instruction to the jury was that if they felt there was enough evidence to prove Coombs had murdered the woman, then they should return a verdict of wilful murder against him, but if there was only suspicion, then they should never hang a man without something to support it. If they could not be sure Coombs was the culprit, then they should return a verdict that the victim met her death at the hands of a person or persons unknown. The jury took only fifteen minutes to return a verdict of murder by an unknown perpetrator.

In 1895 Arthur and Polly married and later left the UK to live in Canada, most likely looking for a fresh start and to escape the suspicions which would always lay before Arthur. the couple never returned and led a long and fruitful life in their new home. The Murderer of Elsie Luke has never been uncovered, she was laid to rest in the area, and a headstone  was paid for by a member of the community as a reminder of her tragic unsolved murder.

Is this story of Elsie Adeline Luke's murder really a mystery? It feels almost impossible to remove the suspicion of Arthur Coombs involvement in Elsie's demise. It is interesting to note that Polly Sheppard's role in this story was never explored further by the police as she, like Arthur, had a motive for her death. Her letters to her sweetheart, whom she knew was unfaithful to her, was full of hate for Elsie and the two women had fought publicly. It is also questionable as to why that bank holiday Monday was specifically identified as the day Elsie died; we know that 5pm that day was the last time she was seen but her skeleton and the forensics of this time would not have been able to prove with certainty that she died on the evening Arthur and Polly were at the Theatre.

Throughout this story, Elsie remains an enigma. Whilst Arthur had a history and many acquaintances in the area, Elsie had none. There was no person in this investigation who could really prove any level of relationship with her, and it seems that while quite a few people gave their accounts of Elsie's movements and what she had told them, no one really seemed to 'know' her. She had laid in that cave for two years before being discovered, and in this time, no one really questioned where she was. It's understandable that her acquaintances in Bath may have accepted her absence with a sigh of relief because she was painted as an uncouth and difficult woman, but it seems unusual that a young woman of whom people said was well spoken and well educated would not be missed by someone in her birthplace of Canning Town, London.

It is also possible that Elsie had other lovers in her life, not just Arthur. Is it possible that Arthur was not the only man Elsie had accused of fathering her child? Had she attempted to cause havoc in another man's life who then took measures to silence her forever?

Did the man who found her jewellery on the downs, Mr Dill, know more than he admitted to? He failed to hand these finds into the police and kept the cufflinks and bloody handkerchief in a safe place for two years. Was this something a man with no connection to an incident would do?

On the surface, this story did not feel such a mystery, with all suspicion pointing toward Arthur and Polly. However, it is understandable that the jury decided they could not condemn a man to face the noose with so many unanswered questions and the absence of real evidence.

Oake Family poisoning

Eli Walter Maunder lived with his wife Emma and six children in the village of Oake near Milverton. Walter, as he was better known, worked at a local farm as an agricultural labourer, and although the family must have lived on a tight income, they had three healthy sons and three healthy daughters. In December 1900, the family were struck down with a mystery illness, and within four days, five members of the family were dead.

On the 10th December 1900, 30 year old Walter went to work at Rendy farm and told co-worker James Fry that his wife Emma, and two of his children were all unwell, he said he himself also felt ill, to which his workmate advised Walter to send for a doctor. Medical practitioner Charles Randolph attended the family home, and after examining them, diagnosed sickness caused by some fish the family had eaten, he began treating them accordingly. On the same evening, Emma Maunder's friend Eliza Broom called at the family home and spoke to Emma, who was very unwell with diarrhoea and vomiting. Emma told Eliza she thought the family's illness was caused by water from a local well which had been thick and discoloured. She told her friend that from now on, the family would only be getting water from the farm.

The following day Walter did not appear at work but later in the evening attended the farm to fetch a jug of water. Walter was so weak he could not carry the water and was helped by a friend. Eliza Broom continued to visit the family, and on the 13th December, she witnessed the death of the couple's two-year-old daughter Lily. Eliza stayed with the family for the next two nights as their health continued to decline. On the 17th December, Dr Randolph returned to the family home to find four members of the family gravely ill. He found that all the children, apart from the baby, were suffering from this mystery illness.

He immediately ordered that Emma and the children be taken to lodgings in Milverton where he could provide better care. Walter had now become so unwell that he was delusional and violent and was sent to the Taunton and Somerset Hospital. He arrived there at 3 pm and died within six hours. Four-year-old Thomas died on the 18th December, and eight-year-old John died two days later, Emma Maunder died on the 21st

December aged only thirty. Annie and James remained in a critical condition while baby Mary Ann, having been breastfed, remained well.

On the 20th December 1900, coroner Mr T Barham opened an inquest into Walter Maunder's death. Thomas Bawden, a local carter, and friend of Walter told the inquest that two weeks ago he and Walter had been riding together when they saw a stoate pursuing a rabbit. Walter had followed the animals and after setting his dog upon the stoate, picked up the rabbit, saying it would make a good family meal. The rabbit had been bitten on the leg and head by the stoate. William Raffle, the family's lodger appeared before the jury and told how on the 8th December the family ate some herring that had been purchased the night before. Everyone apart from Emma and the baby had eaten the fish. Raffles told the court that he had eaten both the herring and the rabbit mentioned by the previous witness and found no peculiar smell. He had not become unwell.

Taunton and Somerset hospital surgeon William Drake next took the stand and said that when Walter Maunder arrived at the hospital, he was in a state of collapse and despite medical treatment he had died there around 9 pm. His post-mortem showed inflammation and distension in the stomach and an enlarged liver. Drake stated that in his opinion, Walter's death was caused by ingestion of poison and that he had sent the stomach contents to Dr Alford, the county analyst, for his opinion. Doctor Randolph, who attended the family told the court that when he visited, he had found the property in an unhygienic condition, with old food left lying around and 'all kinds of filth'. When asked by the coroner about the local water supply, Dr Randolph stated that the water in the local well was dirty and discoloured and he had raised concerns regarding this in the past to which the well was cleaned. He said that although he agreed the water was not fit for human consumption, he did not feel that this had caused the families deaths.

The children's post-mortems were carried out and like their father, inflammation and enlarged organs were found. The children's stomach remains were sent to a specialist in London at the request of the home office, and as with Walter, one grain of arsenic was found in their digestive systems. Examination of the children's stomachs indicated that the arsenic had been consumed with liquid.

The inquest adjourned to allow a further investigation to be carried out, however, when the court convened on the 10th January 1901 no new evidence was found. A thorough search of the family home had found no arsenic. Two bottles of cider found at the property were tested, but no arsenic was found. The local well was checked but had already been cleaned in response to the deaths so offered no new information. Coroner T Barham commented that this was the most incomprehensible affair he had ever dealt with. Once all possible evidence was examined, the coroner told the jury that they had no choice but to return an open verdict. The jury stated that all five deaths were due to arsenic poisonings, but there was no evidence of how or by who this was administered.

The mystery of what or who caused the death of five members of one family was never solved. Rumours in the local area speculated that Walter had threatened to kill himself and the others after an argument with his wife, while others suggested that Emma had been suffering from depression since the birth of Mary Ann and may have killed her family. There was also speculation that a young nephew of the couple had placed arsenic in their tea caddy.

Walter and Emma were laid to rest along with their three children Thomas, John, and Lily at Oake churchyard. Both Annie and James recovered after months in hospital. Annie worked as a servant before marrying a local man in 1911. James went to live with his uncle, and baby Mary Ann was adopted by the Bowley family, where she remained until adulthood.

The Codsend Moor Mystery

On Sunday 8th September 1929, 16-year-old Gwendoline 'Molly' Phillips left her employers at Rock Farm in Exford to visit her family in Cutcombe. Molly, described as a pretty dark-haired girl, told the housekeeper she would be visiting her auntie, five miles away in the village of Cutcombe and would be back by 9 pm to shut the chickens in. Molly was never seen alive again.

Molly worked as a farmhand and had resided at Rock Farm for eighteen months. Her employer Mr Leslie Tucker described her as 'a good of a girl as you could hope to find'. She never came back late, never went to dances on her own and never kept male company. Tucker described her as a robust girl who could look after herself. When she did not return on that Sunday evening, Mr Tucker went to her mother Henrietta Ford, to voice his concern. Thinking that she may have stayed overnight at her aunt's house, Henrietta was not too concerned until she visited the village of Cutcombe the following morning to be told that Molly never arrived. A thorough search of the area began by local police. Molly was a local girl who knew the area well, so to locals, the thought that she could be lost was impossible. After the third day of her absence, people began to suspect foul play, her employer telling the police ' If anyone in a motor car had offered her a lift, I believe she would have accepted, that is what she must have done and was carried away.'

The search party had a good description of Molly. Last seen wearing a long-sleeved blue dress, black shoes, and light blue stockings, she had her spectacles on when she left and was wearing a blue beret. However, the girl could not be found. On the 20th September, the Devon and Somerset Staghounds and local boy scout groups joined the search. Miles and miles of Exmoor moors were searched on foot and on horseback by 200 people. The dense bracken, bogs and coombes thoroughly searched, but no clue was found. A local swimmer, Captain Cox, scoured the local lakes with no result. Her family began to wonder if she had been abducted. Her mother stating to the local press – 'I believe Molly has been forcibly taken away, she was in no trouble at home, and there is no reason she would leave her employment. I'm sure if she were alive, and was able, she would have written to me telling me where she is'. Her sister, who lived and worked in Minehead stated that Molly had recently returned from a short holiday to Gloucester with her step-fathers family and had seemed reluctant to return to work at the farm, but never said why.

On the 26th September police searched the home and farm buildings of her employer, Leslie Tucker, they also searched her mother's address but found no sign of the missing girl or her belongings. A young man that Molly had previously walked out with was also questioned, police were satisfied he was not involved in the disappearance. After a month of searching, the darker nights and damper weather brought the searches for Molly to an end. Her family and the local community were left to wonder what could have happened to this well-liked friendly girl.

Eighteen months later, on the 29th March 1931, local farmer Donald Grant of Hawkington Farm was working with an employee on the cold lonely Codsend moor, near Dunkery hill. The men were burning and clearing grass and bracken when he spotted what he thought was a carcass of a dead sheep poking out of a small bog near a stream. Closer inspection revealed there were human bones protruding from the ground, Mr Grant quickly and discreetly called for the police. By the time they arrived, the evening was setting in, and so the skeleton was guarded all night before being carefully removed and taken to the Minehead Mortuary.

The skeleton still had a pair of black shoes attached and this, along with scraps of clothing confirmed this was the skeleton of Molly Phillips. Superintendent Hallett told the media that it was impossible at this point to rule out foul play and that murder, suicide or an accident were all being considered. Whilst the investigation began, the community voiced their suspicions that Molly knew the area too well to have fallen, that the location was three miles away from the route she should have taken, and that at 3 feet deep, the bog was not deep enough to fall and get stuck. In their minds, an accident was very doubtful.

The inquest into Molly's death was opened in a Minehead schoolroom on 2nd April 1931. The jury was made up of thirteen local men, some of whom knew the girl's family. After the jury was shown photographs of the skeleton in the bog and the surrounding area, Molly's mother Henrietta was called to give evidence. Clearly emotional, the woman wore a black dress and sobbed bitterly as she took the oath. Henrietta told the inquest that Molly had worked away from home since she was 14, she was a heavy set girl who was able to look after herself, and that she was well known in the area, having lived there all her life, Henrietta stated Molly knew her way around the moors. She confirmed to the court that she had identified fragments of cloth, a corset, and a shoulder strap she knew to belong to her daughter. She also confirmed she had viewed a tuft of hair that had been found a few yards away from the skeleton. She stated, 'I have no doubt in my mind that this is Molly- none whatsoever'. The grieving mother was then questioned by Superintendent Hallett, who asked her about the area. Henrietta replied that Molly knew the Hawkington area well as she had lived there as a child, he then went on to ask her about Molly's spectacles which were not found with the skeleton. Henrietta told the court that although Molly needed them and suffered from headaches without them, she would be able to find her way without them, as she had many times in the past when her spectacles were lost. Hallett then asked her about the shoes, asking if Molly would wear these if she were planning to walk across the moor, her mother replied that no, she had heavier brown brogues that she would have worn. The court was then told that the coat Molly had over her arm when she left Rock farm had not been recovered. Concluding her evidence, Henrietta also told the court that a bracelet was missing from her daughter's jewellery box, which she suspected she had been wearing the day she vanished.

Miss Rowle, Rock Farm's housekeeper then stood before the jury. She stated she was the last person to see Molly and that when she left Rock Farm on 2 pm of Sunday 9th September 1929, she seemed in good spirits and said she intended to catch a bus to Cutcombe. When she left, she had her spectacles on, a coat over her arm and was wearing a belt with a buckle that had also not been found with the remains. Miss Rowle confirmed that she was not aware of Molly keeping any male company or knew of no male friends.

Donald Grant, the local man who discovered the remains then relayed his account of the discovery, stating that he also saw fragments of clothes floating on the water around the skeleton and a tuft of brown hair, further from the spot. He said he felt this location was of no danger to anyone local as the bog was only a few feet deep and not filled with water in the summer months. He went on to say the area had many visits in the summer from walkers and those enjoying a picnic and he was surprised the remains could have been there all this time without being spotted. When asked by the superintendent, he stated that to him the remains looked as though they had sunk rather than been buried. Another local man who worked as a rabbit trapper told the jury the area could be deceivingly boggy and that someone with an injured leg may indeed get stuck in the bog and would not be able to free themselves without help.

Dr Carter, the pathologist, then addressed the court describing how the remains were found- lying on its left side with head drooping towards the left chest. The body was pitched forward, and the feet embedded in the turf. Stones were found around the body, including one which sat between the knee and ankle. One arm was thrown upwards. He stated he did not believe that the body was placed there but that Molly was alive when she entered the bog. His examination of the body identified a broken leg but no further injury. His opinion on the case was 'the girl caught her foot on a stone at the edge of the bog, causing her to trip and fall forward, throwing her arms up to save herself. The cause of death was shock from exposure with the possibility of drowning'. He went on to suggest that Molly never intended to leave the road, but someone had frightened her- possibly an assault- that caused her to run across the moor. The jury deliberated for a short time before stating that they agreed with the Doctors theory and returned a verdict of death by misadventure.

The outcome of the inquest outraged many in the local community with so many unanswered questions and many inconsistencies not addressed. When asked by a reporter if he could accept the doctor's theory into the cause of death, Superintendent Hallett replied that he could not answer that question. Cutcombe's local rector Reverend Jenoures was less diplomatic in his opinions stating that 'A great many of us know where the girl's remains were found. Yet we are being asked to believe this feeble story which might as well have been taken from the pages of a nursery book. We are asked to believe that this powerful young woman, who knew the moors well, carelessly ran into a bog which at that time of year probably didn't exist and quietly laid there and died without a struggle to get out'

Fuelled by the rector's comments, local people demanded a public meeting, stating that all that knew the area knew there was no water on that moor in the summer months, that they wanted an explanation as to why there were large stones which they said were placed on top of the body, and a further search to find the girls missing items. Doctor Godfrey Carter responded that he felt the inquest was carried out with great care and there was nothing left to be said about it. The coroner Mr Clarkes told the media that all members of the jury were local men who knew the land and the girl, and this was their verdict. Reverend Jenoures continued to receive complaints from the locals as well as letters from further afield and made the decision to petition the home office to reopen the inquest.

There are varying accounts as to whether Molly's mother agreed to the request to reopen the investigation, initially it was reported she did, but later an MP would state in the House of Commons that she never agreed to this and did not support it. On the 10th April 1931, five West Somerset police officers attended the location where Molly's remains were found and dug in the area for six hours. This was greatly received by locals who said they hoped the missing items, spectacles, a belt, coat, and bracelet would be found. The following day the reverend received a telegram from London, and a woman from Timberscombe came forward to police giving information about a man who was serving a sentence in Exeter prison. This appeared to be a dead lead as no further information was given on this man. The reverend had now sent representation to London, telling the papers that he was satisfied that Molly was murdered as he had attended the bog and measured the area. He recorded that a depth of one foot 6 inches was not deep enough for a thickset girl to get stuck. He told the papers 'I challenge anyone to throw me into the bog and to say that I cannot get out in five minutes. I will give £20 if I cannot do it, I would of course, donate my winnings to the hospital'.

When asked about their search, Mr Bawden, a huntsman of Devon and Somerset staghounds, reported that they had searched the area Molly was subsequently found on the 10th and 12th of September 1929. On the 26th September, over 200 people searched Codsend Moor thoroughly and felt she would have been spotted. He also consulted his records and was able to prove that after a particularly dry summer, no rain had fallen until 1st October, suggesting the area would have been dry and not boggy as the doctor suggested at the inquest.

Attention was also drawn to the tuft of hair that was found away from the body, locals suggesting it had been torn from her head. The community began demanding Molly's body be exhumed, and a more thorough examination carried out. Superintendent Hallett and his team continued to make enquiries to the public and once again appealed to the public that was in the area to think hard again about that day, if they saw anything, suggesting that possibly Molly never intended to visit her aunt that day and had instead made plans with some unknown person. The Inspector spoke of a sailor who had worked with Molly in a previous employment, asking him to come forward for questioning, however no such man ever did.

In May 1931 in an attempt to curb the public and no doubt the rector, the police sought advice from Sir Bernard Spilsbury, renowned London pathologist, to examine the evidence including the tuft of hair, the attorney general stated once they had this report, they would make a decision if the inquest should be reopened.

Later the same month, the attorney general read out a letter he received from Henrietta Ford stating that she did not wish for the case to be reopened, he read her letter aloud in Parliament. 'I do not see that anything else can be done in the matter and certainly I do not wish for the case to be reopened as I can no longer stand it'. A few days later, Sir Spilsbury submitted his report, which stated that the evidence gathered was consistent with an accidental death and not a murder or suicide. He stated the tuft of hair found near the remains had not been torn from her head but had perhaps been moved by a wild animal. He said that hair is one of the longest-lasting parts of a corpse, and that would explain why it was still intact at the scene. He also informed that on the police's search of 10th April Molly's spectacles were found near the site suggesting she fell. He made no comment on the rector's allegation that the skeleton had been missing an arm which was omitted in the inquest. The original Inquest remained in place- Death by Misadventure.

Was Molly Phillips murdered? I think so. There are so many facts in this case which contradict a finding of an accident. Molly had grown up in the area, she knew those moors and she would have known the boggy areas. If she had intended to go across the moors she would have worn sturdier shoes. Many locals, including the vicar, were adamant it was impossible to become stuck or drown in the area her skeleton was found. It seems ironic that the pathologist could state that he felt she was chased or was fleeing from something she was frightened of but then refuse to consider the possibility she was murdered or was taken to this lonely, isolated spot after her death.

Mysterious People

This chapter is dedicated to my favourite thing about Somerset—the people. As a society, we are predictable beasts, we work, we make a home, we rear a family, we accumulate belongings, and eventually, we perish. In general, all our lives follow a pattern as we age. Our loved ones know where we are, who we are, and the path we have taken. But every so often, a person can appear with no explanation. No history, no local connections, and only their word as to who they are. Equally, a person can vanish… without a trace. Leaving their loved ones and the authorities completely baffled. In cities, it may be more plausible that a person simply leaves the area, but in a rural community like Somerset, any disappearance or suspicious new arrivals readily pique the interest of the locals.

In the following pages, there are mysterious skeletons, severed limbs with no body, a foreign woman with no name and no home, an influential bank manager who completely vanishes, and a man who claims to have supernatural gifts to influence one's fate. People that have perished without explanation, have arrived, and wowed a community, or completely vanished, leaving broken hearts and legal entanglements in their wake.

All the stories detailed have some element of mystery which remains unsolved, and at some point, someone somewhere knew the truth…. but kept their secret safe.

Skeletons

It seems inevitable that in a county where there is evidence of at least 13,000 years of human activity, the odd skeleton or historical graveyard will be discovered. Many great resting places along with tools and artefacts have been discovered here which gives us an insight into ancient Somerset.

In December 1903, a remarkable Mesolithic discovery was made in Gough's Cave at Cheddar. A complete skeleton of a male who lived 10,000 years before. He would become known as the Cheddar Man. The hunter-gatherer was five-foot-four and was believed to have died in his 20's, in a seemly violent death. With further advances in DNA, Cheddar Man was studied again at The National History Museum in 2018. Genetic markers indicated this man had dark skin, blue or green eyes, and curly black hair. Just three years later, the skeleton of a female was found in a mine in the village of Priddy. This skeleton was found 16 feet under mud. The woman's jet black hair had been preserved by its surroundings and her plait remained intact.

In the 1960s, over 50 skeletons discovered at Beckery Chapel in Glastonbury were thought to be the earliest significant evidence of monks in the UK. All the skeletons were male apart from one female and two children, leading researchers to believe they had discovered a monastic burial ground. In 2016, a community training dig involving 25 local people uncovered a further two skeletons, which, when carbon dated, were proved to have died between 406-544 AD. In the winter of 2019, 50 skeletons of both adults and children were discovered in a Somerton school site. The burial site was believed to date from around 43 to 410 AD. The skeletons were laid in graves cut into the bedrock and were surrounded by stone curbs which created the effect of a coffin. Archaeologists also discovered pottery and brooches and evidence suggested these people were slaves to their Roman masters and may originally have held a high status before the Roman invasion.

However, there have been incidences of skeletons discovered in the county of much more recent times, of which remain a mystery to this day.

In August 1896, a building contractor made a grisly discovery when carrying out renovations to a recently purchased house called 'The Green' in Somerton. Lifting up a floorboard to lay a pipe in the attic, Mr Albert Dyer discovered a suspicious package wrapped in a woman's apron—the skeleton of an infant. A further search uncovered a further three infants, all laid side by side and all wrapped in aprons or rags. The skeletons were placed in the hands of the coroner and an investigation into the history of the house began.

The Green had been recently purchased by Mr E Valentine, and before that, had been occupied by a Mr Welch, who had lived there throughout his life. Mr Welch was a bachelor and a man of independent means; he had died in the property at the age of 82. In the last 30 years of his life, Mr Welch had lived with his housekeeper, Eliza Edwards. When he passed away, he bequeathed Eliza with a house for her and her son and a generous sum of £100 a year. There had never been any indication of a relationship between the two, however, rumours in the small community were rife of an illicit affair. Eliza Edwards, who now lived nearby, had for some time been deranged in the mind, and due to her fragile state, was not told of the discovery. A local woman who had visited the house on many occasions stated she never noticed an unusual smell or anything amiss at the property.

Dr Wade of Somerton was called on to examine the skeletons. He stated that all the flesh was absent from the body apart from a little skin on the hands and feet. He felt that two of the babies appeared to have been fully developed while two appeared to be premature. He could not confirm the sex of the babies or whether they had been born alive. He could not offer a length of time the remains had been there other than to say it could be 5, 10, or 20 years. He surmised that the body of an infant would become a skeleton much quicker than an adult and that the area the infants were concealed had a good circulation of air, which may speed up the decomposition. A member of the jury commented that the material of the apron had been used a lot around 10 years ago and suggested it should be kept for further analysis. As no explanation could be offered to who the mother of these babies was or how they died, the jury returned an open verdict, and the coroner suggested the skeletons be donated to a museum which was met with some amusement in the courtroom.

Two years later, a similar case occurred in the nearby village of Aller, when two infant skeletons were discovered in the disused attic of Mrs Ann Gent by the housekeeper. The babies had been wrapped in crepe rags secured with tape, and then covered with a black skirt which had gone green with time. The doctor who examined the skeletons said they had been there for at least 20 years and there was no indication of how they died. The coroner decided that due to the circumstances, no inquest was necessary. These babies were most likely to have been the product of an unwanted pregnancy in a time when an unmarried mother would have caused disgrace in the local community.

In 1936, another infant skeleton was found in the wall of a property called Sandhill in Withycombe. Unlike the previous cases, this skeleton was believed to be dated back to the Plantagenet era as the wall it was uncovered in was an original fixture built hundreds of years ago. Some suggested that the child may have been walled in at the house as a sacrifice in return for stability for the family home.

In April 1932, Peter Fitzpatrick, having no home of his own, went into Somerton Hill Woods, a thick wood on the Langport to Somerton road, to find a place to rest for the night. Hoping to find some comfort, he spotted a thicket with what he thought were rags. He considered the rags as perfect to rest his head, but coming closer to the heap, he was startled to discover the cloth was attached to a skeleton which was laid out on its back, its head resting in between the roots of the tree. There was no flesh remaining and the skeleton laid there, still dressed in male dishevelled clothing and wearing a pair of brown boots. Peter immediately went to

Somerton Police Station and returned to the spot with police constable, Henry Pope, who confirmed that this was indeed the skeleton of a full-size human. There were no articles at the site to identify the man, however, the constable felt that the body of the 5'8 man was laid out as if the person had stopped to rest. In the deceased's pocket, he found a razor and a pipe.

The bones were removed to the Langport poor-law institution and were examined by Dr Carter, local pathologist, who deduced that this man would have been around 50 years of age. There were no signs of a violent death to the skeleton. Local police made enquiries to find out if any local men had been reported missing in the last few years but no one came forward with any clues to this man's identity. An inquest was held, and in his summing up, the coroner stated this was a very unsatisfactory case, a skeleton with no identity and no date or cause of death. He advised the jury that they had no option but to return an open verdict and he only hoped more information may come to light in the future. Completing their deliberation, the jury returned with an open verdict, stating, 'A male skeleton found in Somerton Hill Wood on 22nd April 1932, cause of death unknown. The age of the skeleton was in the neighbourhood of 50 years old'. No further mention of this incident occurred and the man remained unknown.

In October 1934, a skeleton of a male was discovered nine feet under a field in Burnham on Sea. Unusually, this skeleton was found in a sitting position with his knees drawn up and his hands at his sides. Further investigation found that the skeleton was that of a young man and had been there for over 50 years. As aged townsfolk could not recall any missing persons in the area 50 years ago, the North Somerset coroner ruled no inquest was required.

Five years later, In August 1939, a fisherman's son, searching for a lost anchor at Sand Bay in Kewstoke had a shock when his spade struck a hard object, which he quickly discovered was a skull. He phoned for the police, who arrived and dug up the remaining skeleton. PC Hansford noted that the skeleton was laid on its back, 40 feet under the water level and adjacent to the shoreline. Astonishingly, the hands and feet of the skeleton were missing. The fisherman's father, Mr Thomas, told how he was employed by the board of trade to bury carcasses of animals that wash up on the beach and that, in his experience,

anything buried ten feet below the surface would not be disturbed by the tide which suggested the body could have been there for a long time.

Sand Bay, Kewstoke

The skeleton was taken for examination and was found to be a five-foot-six-inch male with a well-shaped head. The age of the deceased was estimated at between 30 and 40 and it seemed likely his death took place 20 to 25 years before. The coroner felt that although both hands and feet were missing, this death was not necessarily foul play, and as no missing persons were reported 25 years ago and there was no way to identify the man, a verdict of 'found buried' was recorded.

Just one week later, a tourist hunting for fossils with friends, just a few miles along the coast at Brean Downs, discovered an exposed skull. He and his friends dug up the remaining bones which were six foot under the sand and reported the find to the police. Unlike the skeleton at Kewstoke, this body was found to be centuries old and no inquest was required.

Body Snatchers in Somerset

A rather grim crime from the 17th and 18th century, a body snatcher was officially referred to as a resurrectionist. During this time, dissection of a corpse was a criminal offence on any human other than a hanged criminal. As surgeons continued their research into the human anatomy and how to treat and prevent disease, more medical and anatomical schools opened and the need for dead bodies rapidly surpassed the amount of executions carried out. As the 19th century began and the use of capital punishment was greatly reduced in favour of transportation, these medical schools were in desperate need of cadavers for their research and lectures.

Although dissection was illegal, removing a dead body from its resting place was not. A black market for freshly deceased people quickly grew and the crime of body snatching became a nationwide problem. These resurrectionists normally worked in a team and carried out their macabre crimes during the night for obvious reasons! Contrary to fictional depictions of body snatching, the criminals did not actually bring the whole coffin to the surface, instead, they had adopted methods to complete the task much more efficiently and quickly. A skilled body snatcher could complete the whole task within an hour. The first method was to dig just the area where the deceased's head would rest. After breaking the lid, they would use a hook or rope to pull the body to the surface. Another, more time-consuming method was to dig nearby and tunnel into the location, removing the body by breaking open the coffin at one end. As the sentencing for body snatching was so lax compared to other crimes, the criminals would remove any clothes the departed was wearing and place them back into the coffin, therefore, not committing the crime of stealing attire which could get you transported for seven years! They would then smooth the ground to conceal any disturbance at the resting place.

Once the snatchers had their merchandise, they needed to move quickly. Embalming was not introduced until the 1880s and so a body would only remain fresh for a short time before it would become putrid and useless to the gang.

Resurrectionists at work, Hablot Knight Browne, 1887

Jewish graveyards were preferable if there was one in the area. Jewish custom dictated that the departed should be buried within 24 hours, so the snatchers would be guaranteed more time to move the body before it festered. A team of body snatchers could earn three months labouring wages for just one body; however, surgeons would only accept corpses that were fresh and in good condition, so speed was imperative.

Transporting the body posed its own challenges in smaller rural areas such as Somerset. In the cities, there would have been medical schools within close proximity of the deceased's resting place, but in rural locations, body snatchers would often have to remove body parts or attempt to fold the body to make it easier to transport and send it up to

Bristol or London via the coach services. This posed its very own risks as often the 'package' would start to smell or would leak fluids which raised suspicions. If a body snatcher was not caught in the act at the graveside, then this would normally be how they would be discovered. Criminals would not have enjoyed the anonymity of city life in a small Somerset town. The person who dropped off the package would always be identifiable.

Although not harshly punished in the courts, body snatching was an abominable crime which would break the hearts of family members who had recently lost a loved one. The Victorians had a morbid fear of death and of being misdiagnosed and buried alive. The added concern of being stolen from their resting place and sold to be dissected filled people with a morbid fear. And so, they began taking their own measures to protect their resting loved ones. Wealthier families would hire a watchman to stay at the grave for up to a month after burial, whilst others invested in family tombs and vaults. Less wealthy families could pay to have a metal cage erected or have heavy slabs or metal planks placed across the resting place. For those with a more limited budget, the family would take it in turns to stay at the graveside for nights on end. Some would plant flowers at the head of the grave which would alert them to any disturbance of the ground, while others would place brambles into the earth to make it more difficult for a potential body snatcher to unearth their loved one.

As time went on, devices were invented to deter and even injure a potential grave robber. A coffin collar was an iron collar fixed to a heavy piece of wood which was then fixed to the bottom of the collar. The collar was placed around the deceased's neck, making it impossible to pull the body from its box. Cemetery guns, also referred to as trip guns, were another ingenious method of stopping a body snatcher in his tracks. The guns were positioned over the grave and were rigged with tripwires, these guns fired out stones and sometimes ammunition and were set to aim at the legs. These weapons and other forms of hidden weapons (e.g. for poachers) were banned in the 1820s due to frequent injury caused to innocent people. A clever American man named Phillip K Clover patented the first coffin torpedo in 1878. Like the UK, American graveyards were regularly ransacked by body snatchers. Clover's instrument was similar to a gun, which would be placed in the coffin and loaded with lead bullets that would fire when the lid was removed.

Some parishes began funding a night watchman to patrol the grounds of the churchyards and to protect those laid to rest. This would have been a lonely and eerie job where the watchman would need to patrol the cemetery throughout the night, listening for any movement. There were incidences of these brave men being injured and murdered whilst on duty, although there is no evidence of this in Somerset. Some churches erected watch towers which overlooked the whole cemetery.

The well-known arrests of body snatchers and murderers, Burke and Hare, and the resulting execution of Burke in Scotland in the last two years of the 1820s caused public dismay and many riots. This forced the government to review its policy on dissection and attempt to stamp this illegal trade on human life between criminals and the medical profession. The Anatomy Act of 1832 brought an abolishing of the dissection of hanged prisoners; the act also authorised that any workhouse bodies not claimed within 48 hours could be given to a local surgeon to do as he pleased. The late 1800s brought an end to body snatching as the act of embalming became common practice, preserving a body for a much longer time hence reducing the demand for corpses.

The earliest recorded story of body snatching in Somerset was in 1735 when Alice Hawkeswell was taken from her resting place in West Huntspill. The church warden recorded in the parish records that ten shillings were spent on returning Alice's body from Bridgwater to her home village, three shillings were required to have the body guarded until its return, six shillings for her reburial, five shillings to replace her shroud, and then seven shillings for a guard once she was back in her resting place. Although there is not much detail to this story, it is clear that someone had removed the woman from her grave and was somehow caught.

In March 1826, William Clarke, alias Taylor, stood before the Somerset Assizes accused of stealing four bodies from the Walcot Cemetery near Bath. The court was told that after a suspicious package was found on a coach from Bath to London, William's house in Walcot was searched and three bodies were found packed in hampers, it being apparent these bodies were ready to be sent to their recipient. A further body was found stored in a closet and a large amount of human bones were found in the cellar of the property.

William offered a full and frank confession. He told the court that bad luck had meant he had been engaged in the art of resurrection since he was a six-year-old boy. He claimed that during his criminal career, he had procured over 2000 bodies for medical dissection. When supplies were scarce, he could charge 10 Guineas for a body (equivalent to £700 in today's money). He told the judge he had been arrested for this crime on 28 occasions but had only been tried twice, each time he served a short prison sentence. During his appearance, he expressed that he had the financial burden of a wife and five children to support, he also advocated the use of humans in furthering the medical understanding of the anatomy. He stated he felt this was no different to a recent occasion when an operation the king needed was first practised on three living humans. It was also disclosed in court that he had offered up the body of his own child when he passed through illness to support the further understanding of disease.

William named his two accomplices as William Broadrip and Joseph Madden. He confirmed they had rented a property in Walcot which overlooked the burial ground and the men had stolen 45 bodies over five months. He told the judge that he had been given a guarantee from the medical men that they would step forward if he was ever arrested, but these men had now betrayed him. In his summing up, Justice Burrough expressed his absolute disgust in the prisoners' conduct. He cared not for any opinion that dissection should be tolerated for medical advancement, the law forbids it and his feelings were in accordance with the law of the land. William Clarke was sentenced to 12 months imprisonment and a fine of £100.

In May the following year, William, still in prison, was unable to pay the fine and wrote a letter requesting clemency. The letter was undersigned by 17 members of the college of surgeons in London and supported by the keeper of Ilchester prison. His grounds for a request for clemency were stated as his wife and children were in distress, that he had no hope of paying the fine as they had no money, that he had served his sentence and that his frustration had caused him to attempt to break out of prison on two occasions. Within the petition, the following argument was made:

'The practice of dissecting is essentially necessary to the study and practice of medicine and surgery and as no legal mode exists of procuring bodies for that purpose, your petitioner has been guilty of a crime against the law but has, at his own peril, assisted in the useful object of a profession, whose occupation is the preservation of life and the elevation of human misery'. The outcome of William's plea for clemency has not been found.

Although it cannot be confirmed without doubt, it seems likely that a man named William Jones, arrested in 1829 for the same crime in Bridgwater was in fact, the same man.

In March 1829, the George Inn—hotel and coaching house of Bridgwater—received a wicker basket from a man named Edward Barber. Barber told Mr Sutton, the postmaster, that this was a delicate package containing valuable wine and needed to be handled with the most care. The parcel was to be sent to London on the next available coach. Being aware of its high value, Sutton ordered one of his men to move the basket to a safer location, but as the unsuspecting worker carried the basket, the material broke. Placing his hand inside the package to quickly prevent the contents from falling to the ground, the poor man found himself touching a severed foot. An immediate investigation began and it was quickly ascertained the package had been brought from the home of a man named William Jones in Durleigh. This man had since absconded from the area. The foot was found to belong to a young woman who had recently died during childbirth in Cannington. News of this grisly story confirmed the suspicions of a nearby family whose loved one, Mrs Watkins, had been laid to rest a month before. The grieving family had suspected that Mrs Watkins' grave had been disturbed, the resting place was brought up and indeed the body had vanished. William Jones was arrested in Bristol in the following January. At court, he was sentenced to four months imprisonment for 'disinterring and stealing a dead body'. William Jones (alias Clarke Taylor) was connected to other men in the area who were also arrested and imprisoned, including Joseph Madden, who was later transported for stealing, and John Lawrence who later served a prison sentence for stealing three bodies from a churchyard and storing them in an oil-filled container.

As for the infamous William Jones, the man of many names and many snatchings. Well, he died in Bristol Infirmary in 1831. William bequeathed his body to Doctor Riley, a local surgeon, who he instructed could do as he wished with his body on the condition it was dissected at Lime Kiln Lane Anatomical School in the city and his skeleton preserved. The doctor respectfully carried out William's wishes.

An Extraordinary Sleepy Person

In May 1694, physician William Oliver wrote about an astonishing case he came across in Timsbury near Bath. Samuel Chilton, a twenty five year old healthy labourer fell into a deep sleep in which he remained for one month. When he awoke he stood up, got dressed and went about his business, not uttering a single word for at least a month after. He remained well for years after, until April 1696 when again he fell asleep, refusing to wake for weeks. His family sent for an apothecary from Bath called Mr Gibbs. The apothecary tried all the modern methods of treatment to rouse the man – he bled and blistered him, cupped him, and tried every way to rouse him, staying by his side for over three weeks, the sleeping man never opened his eyes. He remained in his slumber for 10 weeks, his family unable to give him any food or water as he slept with his teeth clenched tight. Seventeen weeks after he fell asleep he woke suddenly, completely oblivious to his months of slumber and refusing to believe it was not the next day as he thought, his mother took him out to the harvest to prove to him that he had slept through the change of season. Although he had been asleep for all this time he was healthy and well and returned to his labouring work. The following year, in August 1697, Samuel once again fell into a deep slumber. This time the family sent for William Oliver, who quickly attended the family home.

On arrival the doctor found Mr Chilton asleep, with a cup of beer, bread, and cheese by his bedside. He bellowed into the ear of man several times but this having no effect tried holding a vial of Ammonia under his nose, resorting to squirting a little up his nostril, which failed to cause any reaction. Seeing no change, Doctor Oliver resorted to pinching his nose, twisting his ears, and holding his hand over his mouth and nose until he almost stopped breathing. The doctor resorted to his last hat trick, stuffing white Hellebore, a plant commonly used at this time for Cholera and Gout, up his nose. Exhausting all ideas, the doctor returned to Bath and sent other medicine men to attempt to rouse the sleeping but seemingly healthy man. The experiments Dr Oliver tried had caused Samuel's nose to become swollen and inflamed and his exasperated family ordered that no more doctors would be allowed to attend.

Samuel Chilton remained in his slumber for three months, rousing on the 19th November 1697 to the relief of his long-suffering mother. She went to him and after her son reassured her he felt fit and well, he immediately slipped back into a deep sleep. In January 1698 Samuel awoke, not able to remember any of the events of the last five months other than to complain to his mother that he had, at times, felt the draught as he slept. He went about his normal life and never suffered from this mystery sleeping ailment again.

The Maid of the Haystack

In 1776, a mysterious woman was discovered living outside in the elements in the village of Flax Bourton near Bristol. The beautiful woman took up a home in the shelter of a hayrick. Some accounts of the story state she remained there for four years while others say nine. The woman decorated the outside of the rick with trinkets and remained there wearing only basic clothing and eating only fruit from the hedges. Intrigued by this beautiful and seemingly vulnerable woman, locals began to offer her food and clothing, she would shy away from any contact with men but began to accept offers of milk and tea from the women of the village. Appearing to prefer her primitive life, she would refuse to accept any warm or fine clothes choosing to live against the elements.

Local playwright and poet, Hannah More, took up the mystery woman's case and gave her the name Louisa. Hannah struck up local interest into the woman's identity and many who had lost daughters came to view her but no one could identify Louisa. Louisa spoke very little, but when she did, she spoke English with a German accent. As the weather turned colder and her health declined, local authorities removed her (with great difficulty) and placed her at St Peter's in Bristol, but witnessing the decline in Louisa's mental health, Hannah bought the hayrick and allowed Louisa to return to live as she chose. Hannah More, also an active philanthropist, was desperate to solve the mystery of this lost soul and wrote a pamphlet entitled 'a Tale of Real Woe', in an effort to raise the public's awareness, hoping someone may recognise her and also to raise money to pay for her care. Enquiries were made across England, France, and Germany but to no avail. Men of different languages were brought to converse with her in the hope they could uncover her history but Louisa remained in her anonymous world in the haystack.

As the years went on, the harsh conditions of living outside on such a limited diet took its toll on Louisa's health and Hannah More persuaded her to go to an asylum in Bristol. Once here, her physical health began to improve but her mind continued to deteriorate.

In January 1782, John Wesley, a Methodist cleric, visited the mysterious woman at the asylum and wrote:

"In the afternoon I called at Mr. Henderson's, at Hanham, and spent some time with poor, disconsolate Louisa. Such a sight, in the space of fourteen years, I never saw before! Pale and wan, worn with sorrow, beaten with wind and rain, having been so long exposed to all weathers, with her hair rough and frizzled, and only a blanket wrapped round her, native beauty gleamed through all.

Her features were small and finely turned; her eyes had a peculiar sweetness; her arms and fingers were delicately shaped, and her voice soft and agreeable. But her understanding was in ruins. She appeared partly insane, partly silly, and childish. She would answer no question concerning herself, only that her name was Louisa. She seemed to take no notice of any person or thing, and seldom spoke above a word or two at a time. Mr. Henderson has restored her health, and she loves him much. She is in a small room by herself and wants nothing that is proper for her…"

The Maid of the Haystack, known as Louisa, remained at the asylum for a long period of time, her stay financed by Hannah More. But no improvement could be made in her mental state and the professionals concluded that she was incurable, having become 'an idiot – now so furious in her behaviour no help could be offered'. The decision was made for the woman to go to St Guy's Hospital in London. Once here, her physical health continued to decline, her slight body ravaged with arthritis from many years of living in the cold and wet wilderness. On the

18th December 1801, Louisa died at St Guy's and was buried in the hospital grounds, all expenses paid by her benefactor, Hannah More.

Image - Louisa, known as 'maid of the haystack'. Engraving by G. Scott, 1805.
Credit: Wellcome Collection

There were many theories as to Louisa's real identity. An engraving of the woman pictured, was commissioned in 1776 by G Scott in an effort to prompt the public's memory, but again, no one came forward with any knowledge of the woman. Some believed she was the illegitimate child of Roman Emperor Francis I, whilst others believed she was the banished Queen of Denmark. Hannah More pursued the more likely notion that the mysterious woman was a lady who had perhaps fled a trauma or had sustained an injury that robbed her of her memory and identity, or perhaps the daughter of a German baron who had disgraced herself. The mystery of the maid of the Haystack has never been solved and continues to baffle historians to this day.

The Disappearance of Owen Parfitt

One of the oldest Somerset mysteries dates back to 1763 and the disappearance of a 70-year-old crippled man from Shepton Mallet. The story was first told in the History and Antiquities of the County of Somerset by John Collinson, which was published in 1793.

The story goes that Owen Parfitt was a 70-year-old who had traded as a tailor in the town of Shepton Mallet. Owen was trained by his father in the family trade but, one morning, he vanished and joined up to fight with the King's army in America and Africa. Locals would describe Owen as a bad-tempered man who told many stories of his misspent youth, travelling the world and partaking in smuggling, piracy, and black magic. When he returned to his hometown, Owen was much disabled, crippled by rheumatism, he returned to live with his sister who was ten years his senior. As his condition worsened, his sister, though aged and feeble herself, took on a caring role for her brother. The siblings received parish relief to finance their needs. Although local people claimed he had fought for his country, Owen never received an army pension but did carry himself with a curt and military manner.

One June afternoon in 1763, the siblings were at their small cottage at Broad Cross, a small turnpike road on the edge of the town. Owen asked his sister if he could sit outside to take some fresh air, and with the help of a younger neighbour called Susannah Snook, they moved the crippled man outside. Dressed in his sleeping dress, they placed him in his chair with a house coat placed around his shoulders. The two women returned inside and Susannah shortly left, leaving her elderly friend making the beds. A short time later, Susannah returned to the Parfitt's to find the old lady bitterly sobbing. She stated that Owen had vanished from his rocking chair and was nowhere to be found, only his house coat remained hanging from the back of the chair. As the village was in the midst of the seasonal haymaking, there were many locals who immediately began searching every lane, street, and field in the local area. All local wells and ponds were also checked but Owen was nowhere to be seen. Later that day, there was heavy rain and a thunderous storm so the search was called off. For many days after his disappearance, the community checked outhouses, ditches, and local roads leading to Wells and Bath but there was no sign of the elderly man. The disappearance of a man who did not have the ability to walk unsupported completely baffled Shepton Mallet. His sister, being 80 years old, could not be suspected of foul play. In her feeble and aged state of health, she would not have been able to exert any kind of force on another nor move and conceal a body. Owen had no savings or worldly goods other than a belt he wore on his body at all times.

The locals had a few theories as to what happened to Owen Parfitt. The most popular assumption was that as Owen had led a wild and dangerous life on the sea as a pirate and he had been carried away by the devil himself during the violent storm. Others offered a less superstitious conclusion that a gang of smugglers had, for a long time, been searching for Owen as he held a secret to hidden loot and they took him, threw him on a cart, and carried him away, however, no strange carts were spotted in the town that day. Some suggested that locals had been paid by these pirates to keep quiet while they took the elderly man from the front of the house. The original storyteller, John Collinson, stated in his account that a man fitting Owen's description had been seen later that day near woods in Frome, and that whilst ambling along, he may have fallen into a pool or cave where he perished. No body was ever found and his sister remained adamant he could not walk any small distance without help.

In 1814, a man named Thomas Strode bought a cottage just 150 yards from the Parfitt's home. Whilst digging up the garden of his new home, he discovered a skeleton. Great excitement embraced the town, was the mystery of Owen Parfitt's mysterious disappearance finally solved? The skeleton was examined and it was ruled that it was actually of a young female in her 20s. New suspicions circulated the area.

Was Owen responsible for this young girl's death? Did the devil come to take him as punishment for his actions?

Was Owen Parfitt a dastardly pirate like Blackbeard?
Depicted here in A general history of Pyrates in 1724.

The discovery of this skeleton prompted local headmaster, Dr Butler of Shrewsbury School, to investigate Owen Parfitt's disappearance once again. There were very few people in the town who still lived to tell the tale, but those who did could only offer the same information they had 50 years before. His sister by this time had passed many years ago. The headmaster drew the same conclusions. No one witnessed Owen leaving the area, his sister cared for him lovingly, there was no sign of a struggle or violence, and the fiery man had no worldly goods of any value. The disappearance of Owen Parfitt remains a mystery.

In an article printed in 1892 in the Shepton Mallet Journal, the writer ridiculed the local suspicions of the wicked man being carried away by the devil. He suggested that Owen Parfitt fought in Africa for his own ends and led a life of criminality that came back to haunt him in the form of a vengeful accomplice from his past. The article also mentioned a woman named widow Lockyer who had previously lived in the cottage where the skeleton of the young woman was found. The widow was rumoured to have had a connection to Owen Parfitt, although it is unclear whether this was through a family link or through affairs of the heart. She was known locally as an unfriendly reclusive woman who shunned her neighbours. She was known to be of bad character and would have lived in the property when the deceased was buried. She had already died when the skeleton was discovered in 1814. Unfortunately, whilst the writer printed a derisive article towards the local's superstitions, he did not provide any sources or evidence for his own theories.

The Radstock Rope Mystery

The Somerset Coalfield is an area in North Somerset covering 240 square miles. Stretching from the Mendip Hills to Nailsea, the area once provided a lucrative supply of coal and employed over 4000 men and boys in the area. The Wellsway pit in Midsomer Norton was a small colliery in comparison to some of the local pits and put food on the table of many local families in the area. In 1839, tragedy struck when an accident at the pit claimed the lives of 12 men and boys. But was it an accident or had someone tampered with the rope?

At 4 am on the morning of the 9th November 1839, 12 workers arrived to start their gruelling shift. The group were made up of Richard Langford, 44, and his two sons, Alfred, 18, and Farnham, aged 16. James Keevil, aged 41, and his two sons, Mark, 15, and James, 14, William Summers, 26, John Bennett, 41, James Pearce, 18, Amos Dando, 13, and Leonard Dowling, aged just 12. The men were attached to the top prior as always, and when full weight was achieved, they were let down the pit, but suddenly, the rope snapped and all 12 were plummeted 756 feet. The men at the top quickly replaced the rope and went down to find all the men dead, only one of the 12 men recognisable, their bodies smashed and dissevered.

The death rocked the local community and left many widows and young children with no income. A subscription was organised in the local area to support them financially at their time of loss. The national newspapers reported that 'some fiend in human form' had maliciously damaged the rope and a reward for £130 was offered for the identity of the perpetrator. But no suspect could be identified.

While rumours that someone had tampered with the rope continued, an inquest was immediately begun by Mr Uphill Esq. George Kingston, bailiff of the coal pit, was present at the accident and told the inquest that the night before he had witnessed seven men go down the pit and that, at this time, the rope was secure and robust, having been recently replaced. He recounted the story of how the 12 men fell to their deaths shortly after being hooked on to go down and that there was no reason to suspect the rope would not cope with the weight. Inspecting the severed rope, which was a flat hemp rope five inches wide and 1/4-inch-thick, he was of the opinion that someone had purposely damaged the rope with some blunt instrument. He felt that the break in the rope was a clean cut with no strands or fraying you would expect from a break caused by weight damage. He suggested that the damage to the rope was consistent with a blow from a crowbar. He went on to tell the inquest that he had left the site at 7 45 pm the night before and can say with certainty the rope was fine at this time, he slept on the colliery grounds and heard no noise during the night. He knew of no ill-feeling between any of the workers and said that he felt everyone got on and worked well together.

Thomas Jones, another man present at the time of the accident, told the inquest that he pulled back the wooden covering of the pit mouth before the men's decline. As the men were about to descend, one of the victims, William Summers, exclaimed there was something wrong with the rope, just as the men fell to their death. The jury returned a verdict of wilful murder by some person or persons unknown

The 12 men and boys were buried alongside each other at Midsomer Norton Church. The funeral was attended by over 4000 local mourners and was described as a deeply distressing day. The coalmasters of Radstock were complimented for their kindness to the families, offering financial and emotional support and providing a headstone in memory of their lost workers. Colonel Bullen, a well-known admiral, suggested changes to the way the colliery workers were transported into the pit and a safety rope was introduced to be positioned alongside the original rope. He also suggested a net which enclosed the basket to catch the men if the rope failed.

The mystery of how the rope became severed has never been solved. Some reporters suggested that the rope had been used to transport more men than it could hold, but locals always held suspicions that the deed was carried out by some person who was never discovered.

A plaque at the site still remains which reads –

'In this grave are deposited the remains of 12 undermentioned sufferers, all of whom were killed at Wells Way Coal Works on the 8th November 1839, by the snapping of the rope as they were on the point of descending into the pit. The rope was generally supposed to have been maliciously cut.'

Wizard of the West

William Brewer was born in the village of Lyng, near Taunton in 1815. His father was a humble shoemaker and William began his working life as a ploughboy. As a bright ambitious lad, he spotted a gap in the market and began making and selling his own clay pipes. Known as Billy the Piper, he travelled around Somerset, North Dorset, and Devon selling his wares and was well-known as a charismatic young man. In 1840, Billy settled in Taunton, opening his own grocery store at Alfred Street. It was at this address that Billy began offering a little extra at the back of his shop.

Billy first began offering his services as 'a wise man' to a select few. He specialised in fortune-telling, love potions, removal of curses, and remedies to heal the sick. Billy, dressed in his eccentric clothes and with wispy curly hair down to his shoulders, invited people to the back of his shop where he listened intently to their troubles and offered affordable timely solutions. In time, Billy the Piper became so well-known as the Wizard of the West that people of all classes would travel from as far as Cardiff and Bristol to seek his help. Visitors attended to have their fortunes told, their cards read, and to buy potions to influence their fate. People would talk of entering the shop disabled and in agonising pain, leaving a short time later, standing straight and feeling as strong as an ox. Others reported experiencing the sound of rattling chains and demonic voices while having their fortunes told.

Although many people of authority in the community were dubious of his powers, Billy was never arrested, as some other fortune-tellers were. Billy always made a point of telling his customers only to pay what they wished to and never to pay him until the task was complete. The man's eccentricity and charisma always guaranteed he received his payment. Billy was known as a kind man, never taking more than a family could afford. A member of the community later said of the man that although he took money for his supposed skills, he was never a greedy man and was very likeable and famous around the area, swanning around the town in his robes, and sometimes wearing a sombrero hat and velvet gloves. The unmarried man that had a love of cats had captured the heart of many local people.

In a county where superstition of being 'overlooked' or cursed was ripe, Billy became extremely popular in the surrounding villages and hamlets. In some places, he even had his own bed made ready for him, which was considered to bring luck to any person who slept there after the great Wizard had slumbered. A key factor to Billy's popularity in the villages was that he would come and stay at the properties which were suspected of being given the evil eye. He frequented many family homes, staying for days at a time, benefiting from the beef and wine of the farmers who were eager for him to remove their current run of bad luck. At the end of his stay, he would proclaim that the house was free of any evil, and having his palm crossed with silver, made his way home. The farmer then reported to locals that his cattle and home had since thrived.

Billy continued offering his mysterious skills into his elderly years, remaining at Alfred Street, and continuing to enjoy his local notoriety. Having lost his luscious locks as an old man, Billy could be seen wearing a badly-fitted wig, his trademark cloaks, and dozens of rings on his fingers. He frequently attended local events and continued to offer concoctions of yarbs to heal the sick and help young maidens secure the man of their dreams with his love potions.

Billy Brewer died on the 28th December 1890, aged 76. Though he had enjoyed a decent income throughout his life, Billy had lived a basic lifestyle and left very little assets other than the shop. At his inquest, his lodger told how Billy's health had been failing for some time and just three weeks ago, he became bedridden, his lodger caring for him until his death. The cause of death was established as natural causes and enquiries needed to be made for his next of kin. The funeral, paid for by the parish, was arranged for New Year's Day, 1891.

Billy Brewer's funeral was as eventful as his life. When the hearse and carriage, paid for by a friend, arrived at Alfred Street, a number of local people gathered to pay their last respects, however, the customary officer of the guardian failed to arrive and the proceedings were held up. After some time waiting around, the bystanders began muttering their disapproval at the delay of the man's last journey and the police officer ordered the coffin to be brought down. This then caused another delay, as no man present was willing to carry him down for fear of Billy's magical abilities. After a short time, two volunteers came forward. Eventually arriving at St James Church, the funeral was again delayed as the absent guardian should have also brought paperwork. Reverend French initially refused to go ahead with the burial, but noting the public's dismay, he conceded. Unfortunately, as before, no man was willing to carry the coffin from the hearse to the grave. Finally, the grave-digger found two passing tramps who, dressed in rags and with bare feet, agreed to carry the coffin for a small fee. Billy Brewer was eventually laid to rest in a funeral that a local stated was carried out 'with less ceremony and less care than would have been bestowed on a favourite dog'.

After Billy's burial, the Taunton Courier acquired a large quantity of letters that Billy had received from people far and wide. While mocking the naivety, spelling, and penmanship of his followers, the newspaper printed a range for the public to read. These included:

A woman from Tiverton:

'There is a person coming to the house that I live in, to work. She is a great enemy of mine. She is coming on Wednesday. Could you manage to prevent her coming? I should feel grateful if you could manage to keep her away all together. I have also a woman enemy in my house. If you could manage to prevent them reigning over me, I should get on quite well. Do please try and keep that woman away on Wednesday'

A North Petherton Woman who believed she was overlooked:

'I have carried out your instructions, but I find it don't affect the parties yet. I still get the fits and the face ache. Now do you think you can recommend any other thing to find them out? as I fancy I want to know who it is that is doing me wrong'

A young lady from Wellington:

'I want someone to help me out of my trouble and I believe you can do it if you like. Sir, I was holding correspondence with a young man, a soldier Sir, for a long time and last March he deserted. I have not heard anything from him since nor any of his friends and I should like to hear from him if I could... And would you show me the man that will be my husband or would you draw out my nativity for me? Sir, there is another young man who will not speak to me. He has walked with me twice and I have drank with him, could you make him speak to me and be my husband if I wished? I believe you can do any of these things if you chose to'.

A widow from Devon:

'Will you be kind enough to write and tell me if there's not something wrong with me and my cattle, for I get nothing but bad luck, everything I take in hand goes wrong. I have lost three big bullocks, besides other things. There seems always to be something bad. I am a widow with a family'.

A young Somerset farmer:

'I cannot make that girl out. She just speaks and that is all. She is more shy than ever. I fancy you must bring her to me, mind that. I cannot get an opportunity of talking to her. Shall I write her a note, I want to know? And will she keep it secret if I write? Do tell me, send me a line, even if it's only five words about it, would you?'

The many letters were accompanied by obscure recipes for potions and instructions for curing everyday ailments such as warts. Whether Billy Brewer had any supernatural powers or not, it seems he did, throughout his lifetime, offer comfort and hope to those who were uncertain of their future.

German Spy or Friendly Neighbour?

When German Count, Conrad Von Hochberg from the royal house of Pless arrived in the beautiful West Somerset area of Old Cleeve around 1907, he was warmly received by locals. The 45-year-old bachelor purchased 247 acres of land and built himself a magnificent country house he named Croydon Hall. Along with the grand manor house, the property boasted Italian inspired gardens and two farms. Offering employment to local people to work on his estate, the count also became involved in local events, enjoyed golf and stag hunting, and was an avid subscriber to the Devon and Somerset Staghounds. He was well-known for being liberal with his money, filling his grand home with rare art and expensive furniture and throwing lavish gatherings. The count had a great love for England and seemed to embrace its way of life with fondness. As well as his Somerset home, he also enjoyed a townhouse in London.

As tensions grew in Europe between his home country and England, the count feared for his safety and told friends that if war broke out, he would have to return to Germany, so when he vanished just a few days before the 4th September 1914, his staff and friends were not surprised. The count also had a brother who shared his love of England, living near London who also made the decision to return to his native country.

However, a neighbour of the count, Sir Gabriel Prior Goldney, in residence at the Manor House in Halse, discovered the count's disappearance and reported it to the chief of police of Somerset. In what some papers called 'a remarkable coup', the police and Sir Goldney went to the count's home and seized the estate. Rather than a coup, it was later suggested the count foretold this would happen, instructing his staff to sell what they can for themselves, it seemed anti-German sentiment was turning a well-loved eccentric count into a potential enemy of the state.

Count Hochberg's disappearance roused the interests of the whole country with newspapers as far as Scotland reporting that the seizure of the house had uncovered an arsenal of weapons, hundreds of gallons of

Croydon Hall, Rodhuish, image supplied by current owners

petrol, and maps, plans, and diagrams of the local coastal area. The count was described as a tall man with a military appearance, clean-shaven, with sallow features and a saturnine expression. The papers reported that he was a cousin of the Kaiser and a spy of high-rank in the Prussian foreign office.

The papers went on to speculate that the count had received many mysterious German visitors to the property before his disappearance and made a habit of only employing German valets, stewards, and butlers. The very design of the house came under scrutiny with speculation that the windows were large so that the count could see any person approaching the house. Allegations that seaweed was laid under the floorboards in an attempt to soundproof the property were printed and that previous visitors reported a nightwatchman was always employed who handled a dozen watchdogs.

Within the community, the beloved count being villainised because of his nationality was unacceptable, and when a newspaper reported that the count had wired his butler to order him to blow up the house, the rector of Old Cleeve felt the need to intervene in this character assassination. Writing to a London publication, Reverend Weigall spoke highly of the count's character as a parishioner and a supporter of local charities. He stated:

'It would, no doubt, be a piece of interesting parochial history if there were any foundation for the rumours that have been flying about – that the count has been playing the part of a mysterious spy, that he received mysterious German visitors, that he had a store of 300 rifles, 7000 gallons of petrol and plans for the coast and defences around Minehead, stored in his mysterious house in the hills, but alas! The future chronicler of Old Cleeve must deny himself the pleasure of recording these facts, for unfortunately they are not true and what is more unfortunate is that there is not even the shallowest visage of foundation for them, they exist only in the poetic and lively imaginations of those who do not know the facts.'

The media took no notice of the rector's letter and continued to whip up paranoia in the minds of the English, even falsely reporting the count's arrest at Dover. As the war continued into 1915, talk of the count's sequestered property continued and allegations of espionage were unabating. In April, a local man of Williton wrote to a newspaper saying the count had been fond of hunting and had proved himself to be a good sportsman who could ride well. He reminisced a number of fetes held at the count's estate, including one of a baby show, in which the writer sarcastically stated that no babies were killed. The local man went on to criticize the media's betrayal of 'a paying guest of England' who was always so fond of the country and was now serving with the German Red Cross in his native country, nursing the wounded, not fighting the battle.

The Somerset constable issued a statement stating that although there was a possibility Count Hochberg was a German spy, there was no evidence to suggest he was. He addressed the rumours circulating in the media about the contents of the house, stating that the true finding at the estate had been three sporting guns and enough fuel to run the three cars the count kept there. No maps or plans to suggest he was planning on setting up a coastal base for the German's forces. As the war drew to an end in 1918, anti-German sentiment continued and in the November, the church at Old Cleeve removed Count Hochberg's coat of arms from the bench ends.

Croydon Hall was still in the hands of the government in 1921 and an advert was placed in the local papers that the property would be auctioned in October by the 'order of the custodians. The sale was then mysteriously cancelled. The following year, people reported spotting the count back in the area, with speculation he had returned to collect his art.

Count Hochberg never returned to England, he died in Berlin in 1924 aged 57. No evidence was ever publicly given that the count or his family were ever involved in wartime espionage. Croydon Hall was purchased by Captain Bridge, brother of Mrs Geoffrey Luttrell of Dunster Castle. Croydon Hall has returned to the spotlight in more recent times with allegations the property was being used as a venue for adult sex parties, the beautiful building is now under new management and will reopen soon as a wedding venue and hotel.

The Lavinia Barker Mystery

Lavinia Barker was a pretty blonde bob-haired woman who lived with her aunt in the village of St Audrie's in West Somerset. At the age of 33, her parents had long since passed and she had one younger brother called Fred. One Thursday evening in August 1927, Lavinia went to bed at around 10 pm, locking her door behind her. The following morning, concerned that she had not come down for breakfast, her aunt went to rouse her and got no answer from her room. She called for help and after breaking the door open, the room was found empty with the bedroom window wide open. Last seen wearing a light grey dress and brown shoes, Lavinia had vanished with no coat or hat, no money, and had recently suffered with a bad knee for which she had been prescribed bed rest. Other than footsteps in the garden, there was no trace of the young woman. Lavinia was never seen alive again.

Lavinia's disappearance was completely out of character and a search of the local area immediately began. Local shepherds, accompanied by their dogs, searched streams, the beach, ditches, and wooded areas but there was no trace of Lavinia. It is not difficult to contemplate the thoughts her family went through in the following months. Had she run away? Did she have a lover her family were not aware of? Had someone taken her?

In November of the same year, a local lad named George Kingston, a shepherd boy of nearby Holford, was up on the Quantocks with a friend searching for missing sheep. Messing about near the Ranscombe area of the woods, the boys began kicking about an old sheep skull they found in a stream. Looking more carefully at the skull, George realised it did not look like a sheep and took it home to his parents. His mother gave it a good wash and showed her husband, who immediately knew this was, in fact, a human skull. A few days later, Mr Kingston took the skull to the local police station and a search of the area ensued. Three days later, a headless scantily-dressed skeleton was found a quarter of a mile from the sight of the skull, in a boggy stream almost completely obscured by undergrowth. Near the body, there was a raincoat, and further along, the police discovered shreds of clothes, including parts of a corset and grey stockings, which her sister-in-law confirmed did belong to Lavinia. The police followed their grisly find with a statement in which they said that if the skull had not been discovered by the lads, her body may never have been found as it was in such a secluded spot, they went on to say that it was likely the head had been detached by a sheepdog or wild animal and moved away naturally. They clearly stated they did not believe a murder had taken place.

The inquest into Lavinia's death was held at Bardlestone Farm in Kilve. The police recounted their find, adding that although the stream seemed too shallow to drown, they believed she slipped into the stream and perished. They again suggested the skull had detached in the fast-flowing stream and had been carried away by an animal. When asked for an explanation as to why her skeleton was partially clothed, the officer replied it was likely the flow of the stream had torn it from the body. Doctor F C Killick gave evidence that he had seen Lavinia the night before she vanished to tend to her knee, which had troubled her since a cycling accident years before. He had ordered her to take a few days bed rest and stated that although she seemed anxious about missing work, she generally seemed to be of a sane mind. Discussing his postmortem examination, he said that he saw no injury to any part of the skeleton except for the knee, which he was aware of. He told the inquest it was impossible to determine the cause of death as all but a small amount of flesh had left the corpse. Lavinia's brother then spoke to the inquest, outlining what happened the night his sister disappeared. He said she was hysterical on the night she was last seen, very fretful about having to be bed bound. As far as Fred was aware, his sister did not have a lover or any apparent problems in her life. Fred also stated that although Lavinia liked to walk across the hills, he felt the condition of her knee would not have allowed her to walk the three miles to the spot her skeleton was discovered. When asked if any females had suffered lunacy in the family, he replied that only one distant aunt had been to an asylum.

The jury faced two options—if they felt the circumstances of Lavinia's demise could not be explained by the natural elements, then they should state an open verdict. However, if they felt it was clear what had happened, they could state death by misadventure. The jury returned a verdict of 'Found Dead – insufficient evidence'.

No one will ever know now why Lavinia climbed out of her window that night, why at age 33, she felt she needed to do that or whether she had secrets of her own. Perhaps someone once knew something. Did someone take the secret of Lavinia's death to the grave or did she slip whilst in a fit of hysterics?

The Mysterious Miss Vining

William Robertson Lidderdale was born in 1856 in Wiltshire, his father was a well-known local doctor and the family were held in high regard in the area. Rather than following his father into the medical profession, William pursued a career in banking. He began as a clerk with Stuckey's bank, and through diligence and hard work, was promoted as the bank manager of the company's branch in Ilminster at the age of 35. Still a bachelor, William lived alone at East Street in Ilminster, he had for a long time been engaged to a young woman named Bessie Chapman, who he was said to be much in love with, changing his will in 1890 to name her as the sole beneficiary, although they were not yet married.

In January 1892, the wedding was booked. The banns were read in the local church and Bessie Chapman, who was born in Berkshire but lived with relatives in Ilminster, began preparing for married life with a man she had loved for a long time. William began preparing his home for his bride to be, redecorating rooms, and adding soft furnishings to make the house welcoming. He booked three weeks off work as an overseas honeymoon to Australia was planned and all was well. On the 7th January 1892, with just one week to go until the wedding, William Lidderdale told his bride he needed to go to London to complete a deal on a property that he was set to inherit from a deceased friend, and that he would return the following day on the early morning mail train.

William set off on a train from Ilminster to Paddington London carrying a small case of clothes and one thousand pounds in paper notes. Staying at the Great Western Hotel, William telegrammed his fiancé just after his arrival:

'Arrived safely, am sending this to Raby in case I should not see my darling tomorrow. As they did not tell me particulars- I fear the will is not signed. Do not be disappointed my darling if we are out of it. I promised you that if ever I saw Miss Vining again, I would tell you and I do so dear at once. She has found out her old lover is dead, and those old duffers of lawyers must have told I was expected so the first person I ran against on getting out of the train was her. I soon told her what she wanted and got rid of her. She knows we are to be married but does not know the date of the wedding. Now my sweet darling just be happy about this. It will be alright. Excuse this haste as I want to start off. Yours Forever, Willie'.

The 'Miss Vining' that William referred to in his message was a past love that he had mentioned to her and his friends but whom they had never met. William previously told friends that Miss Vining was a passionate but difficult woman he had previously been romantically involved with but had since ended the affair. He described her as a wealthy 30-year-old American woman who had, for a long time, held emotional control over him, refusing to accept he had now moved on and even showed friends letters he had received from her, stating she would never allow him to marry another and making threats on his life. He also told a friend that while holidaying with Miss Vining in Margate in 1890, she had caused him to injure his shoulder by pulling the horse and trap towards the edge of a cliff whilst having an argument.

Days passed and as Bessie anxiously awaited her lover's return, he failed to come back. Hopeful that he may return for his wedding, the preparations went on, and on the 14th of January, the heartbroken woman stood at the church, William did not arrive. His brother stated that William was not a strong man, having recently being diagnosed with diabetes. Enquiries were made in London but after booking into the hotel on his arrival, there were no sightings of the man. William failed to attend a meeting he had arranged with a surveyor and the GWR confirmed that although he had purchased a return ticket to London, the return, booked for the 3.30 am mail train, had not been used. Newspapers appealed for any sightings, describing William as a medium height sallow-looking man with sandy hair and moustache, and a stooped walk. As the days went on, enquiries began into William's role at the bank and all investigations confirmed what the community already thought of him, everything was in order and proper, the same was found of his personal financial affairs. Bessie Chapman, supported by friends, sent men to London to search for any information on the disappearance of William and fears grew that Miss Vining may have had a hand in the disappearance of a man who was described as diligent and held in high esteem in his community.

On the 11th February, a disturbing announcement was found in the obituary column of the Daily Telegraph. It read:

'On Jan 30th on miss B A Vining's yacht foresight, William Robertson Lidderdale of Ilminster. Result of accident on Jan 8th, alighting from carriage when in motion'.

This sudden and mysterious announcement of the man's death caused great concern amongst his friends and family and Scotland Yard had now become involved in the search for the man. An advert was placed in the evening standard requesting Miss Vining to come forward to provide evidence of the death: 'Miss B A H Vining is urgently requested to communicate details of the death of W R Lidderdale on board her yacht Foresight, to his relatives or to Messrs Pritchard and Mitchell of London'.

No one came forward, and enquiries into the original obituary notice uncovered that the advertisement was placed in the post box after closing hours at the newspaper office. Written on the back of the request was the name and address of Miss Vining, Queen Anne Mansions, Westminster. Enquiries proved that no woman of this name ever lived in that building and a search of the Lloyd's registry found no listing of a yacht named Foresight, which coincidentally was the Lidderdale family motto – Foresight is All.

As the weeks went on, the case continued to intrigue the nation, the newspapers speculating he had eloped with this mysterious lover, whilst loved ones of William Lidderdale feared he was held hostage somewhere on a yacht, in the middle of the sea with a spiteful jilted lover. A reward of £25 was offered and some came forward, but their sightings remained unproved and fruitless. One morning in March, Bessie Chapman, still desperate for any news of William, received a large package in the post. The delivery comprised of £500 in paper notes, a jubilee sixpence she knew to be William's, and a visiting card printed for a Miss Vining, with the words 'was true to you' written on the back in William's handwriting. This fuelled speculation that William and Miss Vining had left the country and sightings began being reported in Europe, all of which were unsubstantiated.

Fifteen years later, William Lidderdale remained vanished and Miss Betty Chapman remained a spinster, still hoping that her lover may reappear. In November 1907, his family approached the probate court requesting that William Robertson Lidderdale be presumed dead, having not been sighted since January 1892. William had left a considerable estate, two life insurance policies, shares in the Ilminster Gas Company, and property. All of which was bequeathed to Miss Chapman. The case was heard by Justice Deane, and the insurance companies argued that it was improper to be asked to pay out a life insurance policy on a man not actually proved to be dead. The justice agreed, stating that he felt it was more likely that William had left the country with Miss Vining and that he was very much still alive somewhere in the world. He suggested that William may have placed the advertisement about his own death to alleviate the worry Miss Chapman would have experienced and also so he could repay her for the heartache he had caused by allowing her to claim on the estate. He ordered an adjournment of six months so that more enquiries into the identity and location of Miss Vining could be carried out.

The following month, the solicitor stated that they had new information of a painful nature which could clear up the case once and for all, he also implied that 'Miss Vining' was, in fact, created in the mind of William Lidderdale and that his disappearance was deliberate because he no longer wanted to marry. Elsewhere, witnesses in Somerset came forward to say they remembered a young girl in the town of Shepton Mallet at the same time William was training in the town's bank. The woman was described as a very well-read attractive girl with beautiful golden hair who kept house for her father, having lost her mother in childhood. Although they could not be sure of her name, they were sure that some kind of relationship took place between the two, and that she disappeared from the area shortly before William moved to Ilminster. On the 30th October 1908, the case was thrown out of court.

In February 1910, the case came to court once more, again in front of Justice Deane. The family solicitor, this time, provided evidence of William Lidderdale having been diagnosed with diabetes with a prediction of only four to five years survival, stating to the court that this proved he must be dead by now. However, Justice Deane stated that if his brother really believed William had died five years after his disappearance, then why would he wait 15 years to bring it to probate. He again highlighted the mystery around Miss Vining and her yacht. The judge told the solicitor that William had shown a photograph of the mystery woman to a colleague at the bank. Further to this, a cousin of the missing man could testify he had seen a yacht called Foresight when William had holidayed in Margate in September 1890. The cousin's account confirmed William's earlier story that he had worn a sling as a result of an accident caused by Miss Vining's temper. The justice also questioned the money William had taken to London, stating that if he was to assume £500 of this money was sent to Miss Chapman, then where was the remaining money? He indignantly stated that if no absolute proof of death could be provided, then the case would withstand until there was no natural possibility the man could be alive.

The case appeared again before the court numerous times in the years to come, but as there was no definitive proof of William Lidderdale's death and the mystery of whether Miss Vining was indeed an ex-lover of the man or just a figment of his imagination remained, the case could not be settled.

In 1946, The Taunton Courier reported that a box of cedar had been sold in Kent which may shed some light into where Mr Lidderdale had gone. The box of cedar was sold to a man who fitted the furniture together to reveal a beautiful oriental sideboard. On each piece of cedar, the words 'W.R Lidderdale 1896' were engraved. Did William Lidderdale go to the middle east? No further information was discovered.

In April 1961, journalist, Len Knott, interviewed 80-year-old Bessie Chapman who had never married and still, even after 54 years, hoped she may discover what happened to the love of her life. In the article, Mr Knott portrays Lidderdale as a liar who faked his own death to escape marriage, but even in his scepticism into the man's disappearance, he questions the circumstances. If William Lidderdale was intending to disappear, why didn't he clear his bank account? He withdrew a thousand pounds but left hundreds behind. If he created Miss Vining in his mind, who was the photograph of the woman he had shown a colleague? Would he really have made visiting cards in the name of Miss Vining? With the national coverage, wouldn't a printer have come forward to prove he had been given this job?

The mystery of the disappearance of William Lidderdale was never solved, no body or death certificate was ever produced, and to this day, Mr Lidderdale's fate and Miss Vining's identity remains a mystery.

Further reading

Somerset Executions

Explore Somerset's condemned, their circumstances and how society attributed their conviction and execution.

This book hopes to provide the reader with accounts from across Somerset from the Beautiful city of Bath to the small picturesque town of Ilminster.

There are over thirty true accounts of Somerset Executions, From Murderers to Highwaymen, Forgers to arsonists.

Explore the execution locations of Somerset- from Stonegallows, Ilchester and Shepton Mallet

Read about brutal execution types ranging from the hanging from an old oak tree, burning on the stake to the US army firing squad Meet the professional executioners who crafted and improved the hanging process offering the condemned a dignified death and those that weren't quite so good at their job.

Available from Amazon, my blog amgouldsomersetauthor.com, and local bookstores.

Printed in Great Britain
by Amazon

43646010R00111